Skye Camanachd

A Century Remembered

Martin Macdonald

Skye Camanachd, Portree

First published in 1992 by
SKYE CAMANACHD
Portree
Isle of Skye

British Library Cataloguing in Publication Data
A catalogue record for this book is available from the British Library
ISBN 0 9519523 0 7

Complete origination by Hiscan, Inverness
Printed by Highland Printers, Inverness

do ar muinntir
for our people

Preface

A word about the making of this book. Most of the information for the early chapters comes from the contemporary newspaper reports, supplemented from World War 1 onwards by the memories of those involved. A list of those who gave so hospitably of their time and information can be found overleaf. While the first half of the book contains fairly detailed match reports, only major games are noted for the last 20 years. The main reason is that Skye now play more games in one season than the early teams did over a 20-year period and, in any case, the recent years have been fully reported in the columns of the *West Highland Free Press* and are thus accessible. I have followed the convention, which Highland newspapers used earlier this century, of using a small letter after the prefix "Mac", unless I am quoting from other sources, or am certain that a capital is used. My apologies to those who prefer a capital, but at this distance in time and with a cast of hundreds, it is simply impossible to check what form the people themselves used. My apologies also to the Alasdairs, Alistairs, Alisters, Ians, Iains, etc, who find the wrong version of their names; the same reason applies. Apart from the informants listed overleaf I am grateful to professional colleagues for help and advice freely given. They include Tommy Mackenzie, Portree, for the cover illustration; John Paul, Inverness, Willie Urquhart of the *West Highland Free Press,* and Calum Neish, Skye for the use of their pictures; and the staff of the reference section of Inverness Library, and particularly Michelle Williams, for their help in copying newspaper reports. I would like to thank Ray Michie, MP, for allowing me to quote from the memoirs of her father, Lord Bannerman, and also Sorley Maclean for the use of his poem, An t-Earrach, 1937.

My gratitude goes to Skye Camanachd for offering me this opportunity of making a contribution to the history of our people. It is an ambitious publication for an organisation like a shinty club to undertake, and I should thank the publication committee — Kenny Mackay, Archie Macdonald, Alistair Bruce and Donnie Mackinnon — for their constant support. Donnie Mackinnon requires a special mention. Over the past two years we have travelled much of Scotland, and enjoyed many people's hospitality, in search of information. He has lived every sentence of this book as much as I have — researching, cajoling, encouraging, and cracking the editorial whip when necessary to ensure the impetus was kept up. It is a tribute to his diligence and commitment that it should appear.

Finally, I should thank my wife and family for tolerating the inevitable domestic disruption of the past two months. She is probably now rather grateful that her native Uist allowed shinty to lapse!

Martin Macdonald, Inverness, May 1992

Acknowledgments

Martin Macdonald and Skye Camanachd are grateful to the following people for so freely providing help and information.

Willie Batchen, Foyers; Kenny MacMaster, Strathpeffer; George Cumming, Nairn; Sandy Cumming, Inverness; Hugh Barron, Inverness; Duncan Maclennan, Inverness; Hugh Dan Maclennan, Inverness; Mrs W M Barker, Fortrose; Col Angus Fairrie, Inverness; Jack Richmond, Newtonmore; G Y Slater, Oban; Tommy Nicolson, Tighnabruaich; the late Donald (Dan) Macdonald, Garelochhead; Mrs J Robertson, Edinburgh; Calum Maclean, Glasgow; Roddy Nicolson, Glasgow; Archie Fraser, Glasgow; Duncan Macleod, Glasgow; Willie Macpherson, Glasgow; Donnie (Keeper) Mackenzie, Lochcarron; John Mackenzie, Lochcarron; Allan Campbell, Calgary; Archie Macdonald, Tarscavaig; Angus J Beaton, Tarscavaig; John Macinnes, Tarscavaig; Mrs D Grant, Isleornsay; Murdo Macdonald, Breakish; Mrs H Robertson, Breakish; Calum Robertson, Broadford; Mrs F Campbell, Sconser; Sorley Maclean, Braes; D R Macdonald, Braes; Kenny Macpherson, Braes; the late Alistair (Lala) Mackenzie, Portree; Donald Angie Macleod, Portree; Hamish Macintyre, Portree; John Davidson, Portree; Donald Mackinnon, Portree; Billy Mackinnon, Portree; Miss Catherine Nicolson, Portree; Ian Macdougall, Portree; Andrew Macpherson, Portree; Donald Macleod, Achachore; James Sutherland, Bernisdale; Dr Alasdair Maclean, Bernisdale; Andrew Nicolson, Bernisdale; Alec Mackillop, Knott; Maj Ian Stewart, Skeabost; Maj John Macdonald, Tote.

Skye Camanachd are grateful to the following individuals, companies and organisations for financial support for this book. Only their generosity has made its publication possible.

Skye and Lochalsh Enterprise
Skye and Lochalsh District Council
Skye and Lochalsh Sports Council
Highland Regional Council Gaelic Committee
Highland Regional Council Libraries and
  Leisure Services Department
Glasgow Skye Association
Portree Builders Limited
Macdonald Brothers
Angus Macphie Builders Limited
Mackays Building Supplies
Caberfeidh Electrics
Ewen MacRae (West End Garage) Limited
Portree Coachworks
Sutherlands Garage
Portree Filling Station
Macleod Hotels Limited
Portree Hotel
Skeabost Hotel
Tongadale Hotel
Sligachan Hotel
Cluanie Inn
West Highland Publishing Company Limited
The Corner Shop
Hamish and Iain Macintyre
D A Macleod (Chemist)
Douglas Mackenzie (Bakers)

Alistair Mackenzie (Electrics)
Campbell Stuart and Maclennan
Anderson MacArthur and Company
Donald MacIver and Company
Catriona Macleod and Associates
Alister Mackinnon and Company
Royal Insurance
Inverness Insurance Centre
Prudential Assurance Company
Glenmorangie
Iain and Neil MacFarlane
Donald MacRae (Joiner)
Billy Mackinnon
Jimmy Devlin
Caley Nicolson, Borve
Roddy Nicolson, Borve / Glasgow
Arthur Cormack
Drew Millar
Michie Family, Camustianavaig
Donald Ferguson
Dan Corrigal
John Mackinnon (Crossal)
Norman and Donnie Macleod
Ewen Grant
Bill Young
Rodger Jagger
Kenny Campbell, Penifiler.

Chieftain's Foreword

It is good news indeed that Martin Macdonald has written a book about shinty in Skye. The game has attracted a good deal of attention lately but to have a book about Skye shinty is an added bonus.

A word of sympathy in passing for the followers of the game. Buffeted by the wind, lashed by wintry showers of hail or sleet, still they stand on the sidelines, the elderly to shout criticism or encouragement, the young, caman in hand eagerly awaiting their time to be one of the team out there in the heat of the action.

The game has had its ups and downs over the years but at present with teams springing up in different parts of the island Skye Camanachd will have a broad base from which to select future teams. The foundation for future successes is being laid just now.

How greatly this would have pleased these former players now gone from us, these wizards with stick and ball. We remember them with awe and affection.

How will boys in the future look back to the present time? With awe and wonder perhaps, asking themselves whether they in turn can emulate their fathers and grandfathers? Can they too win the Camanachd Cup?

Cuimhnich air na daoine bho'n tainig sibh - Remember the people you belong to.

Margaret Macpherson,

Portree, May 1992

Contents

Bannocks and cheese 1

Portree to the fore 9

Onward to the Cup 25

Storms and controversy 35

The Robertson Cup 45

The Glasgow Skye 55

Back to the fray 63

Challenging for honours 73

Home again! 81

Fraser Cup and Skeabost Horn...91

Braes, Bernisdale, Sleat, Portree 101

Lochcarron . . . and a cup 109

Farewell to 'The Skye' 121

A fitting finale..125

Chapter 1

Bannocks and cheese

On New Year's Eve 1875 Mairi Mhor nan Oran, the Skye bardess, was in nostalgic mood. As she sat with a group of fellow-Gaels in Glasgow, busily baking the bannocks that would sustain 60 stalwart Highlanders through next day's festive shinty match in the Queen's Park, her mind went back to her childhood in Skeabost.

Next day's game would recall the great days when the whole populace of Skeabost and Carbost used to crowd down to the "*bugha mor*" by the river — she wrote to her friend, John Maclean, Bernisdale — "*le buideal air gach ceann dhe'n raon, agus pailteas bhonnach agus caise*.....with a keg at each end of the field, and plenty of bannocks and cheese." As a child, some 40 and more years earlier, she had probably watched her mother and the women of the townships prepare the bannocks and cheese, much as she was doing at that moment. And filling the kegs — and indeed emptying them! — was no doubt a matter for the men.

The "*bugha mor*", that wide loop of green sward by the Skeabost river, has seen many games of shinty since. But how many of them matched the great communal occasions that Mairi Mhor remembered so warmly from her youth? They belonged to the Gaelic tradition once common throughout the Highlands when whole communities, from the toddler to the aged, turned out on high days and holidays to centre their celebrations around the skills of caman and ball.

Most of these games took place around New Year or Old New Year, on 12 January, which was still celebrated in many parts of the Highlands well into this century. The rules varied according to locality. In some places — perhaps at Skeabost where the river boundaries of the field imposed a certain discipline on the game — two captains would choose teams whose numbers were limited only by the supply of the willing and able-bodied. In others, traditional rivalry between neighbouring communities would dictate the sides and the action might stretch across several miles.

Dan MacDonald from Bernisdale, a notable pre-war Glasgow Skye player, could remember oldtimers earlier this century speak of such games between Bernisdale and Edinbane in their parents' time. "They didn't have goals. They would drive the ball back and fore across the crofts until they reached a certain place, like a boundary wall perhaps," he recalled, "and then they would say '*Chaidh i tigh*'....'It went home' or something like that but '*tigh*' was the word they used."

Clearly such cross-country rampages, with the leading players driving the ball with one hand on the caman and the other fending off opponents, and the pack

Mairi Mhor nan Oran (Great Mary of the Songs) was born in Skeabost in March 1821. Her father, John Macdonald or Iain Ban mac Aonghais Oig (Fair John, son of Young Angus), was a crofter. She married Isaac Macpherson, an Inverness shoemaker, and following his death in 1871 took up nursing to support her family. Following an accusation of theft of an item of clothing she served a prison sentence, though she and her many friends always maintained her innocence. She poured her bitterness over this incident into the poetry she began to compose when well over 50. Mairi Mhor is the best loved of all Skye bards. Her songs show her love of the island and its people, and she took an active part in the political campaigns of the 1880s, frequently appearing on Land League platforms throughout the Highlands. Following a period in Glasgow she returned to Skye in 1882, where she was given a rent-free cottage by Lachlan Macdonald of Skeabost. He also helped with the cost of publishing her poetry in 1891. Mairi Mhor died in the old Temperance Hotel, on Beaumont Crescent, Portree in November 1898.

hot on their heels in support, bore little resemblance to the disciplined game we
know today. But, few and basic though they may have been, there were rules.
One that Dan could recall was contained in the injunction *"Seas do sheas"*, or
"Stand by your stance" in rough translation. "You weren't allowed to turn with
the ball," he explained. "If you started off with the ball on one side of you, you
had to carry on with it on that side, rather like hockey nowadays."

Such occasions, joyous celebrations of communal loyalty and friendly rivalry
among people who knew each other well, were once common throughout Skye.
In townships from Rudha Hunais to Aird Shleibhte the winter dusk would ring
with the cries of the caman players: bannocks and cheese would be shared and
toasts would be drunk. And yet on that New Year when Mairi Mhor relived her
youth in her Glasgow exile few games, if any, would be played in her native
island.

Under the pressure of social and economic circumstances shinty had all but
died out in some parts of the island, and maintained only a flickering and precarious presence in others. As early as 1841, when Mairi Mhor was 20, the parish
minister of Diurinish noted in the Statistical Account that "all public gatherings,
whether for shinty playing, or throwing the putting-stone, for drinking and dancing, for marriages or funerals, have been discontinued, and people live very much
apart."

There were a number of reasons for this and Mairi Mhor certainly pinpointed
one of them in a simple verse:—

Bho'n chaill sinn am fearann
Gun chaill sinn an iomain
S cha mhor gu bheil duin' ann tha eolach oirr'.

Since we lost our land
We lost shinty as well
And there are few men left who are skilful now.

The evictions and clearances, which left vast tracts under sheep in the early
nineteenth century and dispersed thousands of Skye people to the slums of
Glasgow or the far ends of the earth, also dissipated their traditional skills. And
communal life for those who remained, now crammed onto half-acre plots of
infertile land by the shore, was utterly dislocated. Few of the native tacksmen,
who traditionally gave leadership in social events like shinty as in so much else,
still lived on the island, and fewer still made common cause with the people.

The famine years in the middle of the century, particularly between 1846 and
1852, added to the misery. Three-quarters of the people were on the brink of
starvation, existing on a thin diet of shellfish and oatmeal. A dispirited, down-
trodden and fever-ridden population had little reason to celebrate and less
energy for shinty.

The other element in the demise of shinty, and probably the one foremost in
the Diurinish minister's mind as he penned his report, was religious. As waves of

fundamentalist, evangelical zeal swept the island in the early part of the century shinty was assigned to the Devil as surely as fiddling and piping, probably because of its associations with drinking and communal revelry.

"Tha'n sluagh air fas cho iongantach, 's gur cruithneachd leotha bron...," was how Mairi Mhor summed up this strange, new mood. "The people have grown so peculiar that gloom is the wheat they live on...." Although she herself was loyal to the new Free Church, and an ardent follower of Maighstir Ruairidh MacLeod, the famous minister of Bracadale and Snizort who led most of Skye into that church at the Disruption in 1843, she was no friend of gloom and despondency and never wavered in her loyalty to shinty. But Maighstir Ruairidh was proud to boast: "I have raised the standard against shinty and tobacco both, and with some measure of success."

Maighstir Ruairidh was a charismatic and influential figure in nineteenth century Skye. A man of patent integrity, his was one of the few voices raised against the policies of eviction and emigration and the creation of sheep runs, and he won the love and respect of the ordinary people, whatever reservations some of them might have about the narrower aspects of his creed. So he had a right to expect "some measure of success" in his crusades, though he may have overestimated the degree of success.

Certainly his leading elder, Gilleasbuig Gillies, stood the ban on tobacco for about a week before coming to a unilateral decision that an occasional, contemplative pipeful might not be an offence to his Creator! And on long, cold journeys to communion seasons other elders were known to sit in a wayside inn supping a medicinal whisky under Maighstir Ruairidh's baleful gaze as he enjoyed — or pretended to — his lemonade. So also one might imagine that independent-minded crofters might occasionally cut a caman and *"cnapag"* (Mairi Mhor's word for a ball) from a hazel root for their sons, as their fathers had done for them, reasoning that the sight of young lads at play, innocent of all unseemly revelry, would not incur the wrath of the church. As long, of course, as they did not play too blatantly, too loudly, or too near the Sabbath!

Whatever the case, shinty does not seem to have died completely for any great length of time throughout the whole island. Although there is no evidence of any one locality where the tradition flourished from year to year — such as Badenoch, Glenurquhart or Lovat on the mainland, with their advantages of stable communities and resident landlords — there is evidence of sporadic revivals, largely, it should be said, sponsored by sympathetic local gentry.

Thus in January 1850 the *Glasgow Citizen* reported that on Old New Year's Day Patrick Cooper, Lord Macdonald's chamberlain, "desirous of reviving the old sports of the season" had attended a shinty match in Portree. After Mr Cooper had done the honours with refreshments all round the game was resumed with "great spirit and hilarity" until late in the afternoon. "Meetings of this kind, where all classes mingle, must have a beneficial effect," the *Citizen* reporter observed, "and tend to strengthen the feeling of mutual good-will at present existing between Lord Macdonald and the inhabitants of Portree."

Had they read it, this latter comment must have raised eyebrows among the local citizenry, a fair number of whom had been turfed out when the Macdonald Estates cleared the populous townships of Scorrybreck only ten years earlier. Some of them were still living in poor hovels on the edge of the village, others had been dumped in the overcrowded Braes townships. In fact, the whole incident was bizarre. At that time Mr Cooper and his colleagues were actively contemplating further clearances in Strath, and he had ambitious plans for giving "southern" farmers large holdings in every crofting township on the estate, ostensibly to teach the locals how to farm though the crofters were convinced it was to squeeze them out once and for all.

Fortunately, Mr Cooper had to hightail it out of Skye before his plans came to anything, though the Strath clearances did take place. The verdict must be that Maighstir Ruairidh, by standing against clearances and teaching his fellow islanders a degree of self-reliance, did more for shinty in the long run — however sinful the caman in his eyes! — than Patrick Cooper's dubious exercise in public relations on behalf of a remote landlord.

ARNISORT, SKYE, 17th JAN, 1866 - Last Saturday being Old New-year's day, the usual amusements and modes of celebrating it were deferred until Monday; and, according to an invitation by Mr Macleod of Grishornish, a large body of the active and athletic young men from among his tenants and others in this district, to the number of about two hundred, assembled on the green grounds of Coishletter to play at the game of shinty. There was excellent sport, kept up with good spirit, assisted by an ample supply of Highland whisky and other liquors, and a substantial lunch supplied by Mr Macleod. A piper was also present, which afforded the youths an opportunity of varying their sport by dancing reels. A party from Dunvegan Castle was present part of the time, and Mr Macleod, in his usual hospitable manner, entertained the gentlemen to dinner at Grishornish House after the day's sport was over.

Inverness Courier - 25/01/66

SKYE - NOTES FROM TROTTERNISH - On Kilmuir Common, on the 13th inst, a considerable number of young men played a shinty match, which was well contested and very amusing to witness. The vigour and skill displayed on the occasion, under the leadership of Samuel Macleod and Charles Stewart, natives of the place, were astonishing to a bystander, and if the whole band was under the guidance or superintendence of some of our principal gentry and tenant farmers, they could compete with any number of the same class from a distance. They were strong, able, stalwart fellows.

Inverness Courier - 20/01/81

But not all landlords should be tarred with the same brush and some of the shinty revivals have a genuine ring. Mairi Mhor, then raising a family in Inverness, might have been proud to have followed Mr Macleod of Greshornish onto "the green grounds of Coishletter" near Edinbane in January 1866. Sustained by "an ample supply of Highland whisky" and a "substantial lunch" some 200 "athletic young men" had an excellent day's shinty. The game had been held over until Monday from Old New Year's Day which fell on a Saturday, no doubt to avoid encroaching on preparations for the Sabbath.

By January 1881 the Portree correspondent of the *Inverness Courier* was wistfully lamenting the lack of any activity on Old New Year's Day, while observing that "a few years back a shinty match used to take place, but on account of the absence of our townsman, Mr Harry Macdonald of Viewfield, in India, there was no person who took any interest in the matter....." Without the leadership of the local gentry social activity tended to lapse, it seems. But that was soon to change.

From Kilmuir in the same month came a somewhat similar tale of seasonal woe. "These days used to be celebrated by shinty matches, balls, &c, but there is hardly anything of this kind in the district now." But at least the Kilmuir correspondent did have one match to report — played on Kilmuir Common by "strong, able, stalwart fellows" who had clearly organised the affair themselves. "If the whole band was under the guidance or superintendence of some of our principal gentry and tenant farmers, they could compete with any number of the same class from a distance," the correspondent observed, tipping his cap to the said gentry.

But the crofters of the Kilmuir estate, having suffered the rack-renting of Captain William Fraser for 25 years, were in no mood to follow a landlord. That same winter the tenants of the townships of Valtos and Ellishader announced they were withholding their rents. The spark of rebellion quickly spread to the rest of the estate, and to the districts of Glendale and Braes, where the crofters were suffering under similarly oppressive regimes. For the next six years Skye was to be the main cockpit of the land agitation that spread throughout the Highlands, leading to frequent physical confrontation between crofters and the authorities. The hated figure of Sheriff Ivory stalked the island at the head of a reluctant police force — who hated being cast in a political role — arresting crofters on the slightest pretext. In November 1884 two gunboats and a troopship with 350 Royal Marines on board were sent to Skye to "pacify" the islanders, and in October 1886 the Marines returned to an island still in turmoil, where public administration had all but broken down because of a rates strike. Samuel Macleod, who had captained one of the teams that celebrated New Year 1881 on the open fields of Kilmuir, was among the contingent of Bornaskitaig crofters serving three months imprisonment in the Calton Jail as the bells of Edinburgh chimed in New Year 1887.

During those tumultuous years, with the island under the constant scrutiny of the local and national press, no shinty reports are to be found in the papers; if occasional games did take place they were not reported. But it is more than likely that, under the stress of events and explosive political tensions, the sport lapsed completely for a period, much as it had done earlier in the century in the face of famine, clearance or a frown from the pulpit. After all it is rather difficult to organise a shinty match if a crofter revolt is likely to erupt at any moment as a rival attraction, or half your pool of players is in gaol!

But as the tensions died slowly, and the island began to return to some semblance of normality when the provisions of the 1886 Crofters Act began to take effect, shinty began to revive. The first hint of a new spring was in Sleat, a backwater almost untouched by the active skirmishing of the land war. On Old New Year's Day 1887 in a field near Armadale Castle, with Mr Donald Macdonald of Tormore as main promoter, a team from Aird defeated a Calgary team 4-0 in a three-hour, 30-a-side tussle that only ended with the onset of dusk. The teams were sustained in their marathon bout by "refreshments provided at intervals throughout the day by Mr Macdonald."

Two years later on the same day "camanachd was carried on with great zest in a park adjoining Knock Lodge by a large number of the young men and boys in the vicinity," the *Oban Times* reported. "Captain Kemble of the Lodge took considerable interest in the matches, and invited the whole party to the Lodge, where a liberal supply of refreshments was given to the grown-up men, and tea and fruit with accompaniments to the boys....." The old tradition of festive shinty had re-established itself in Sleat and was to continue largely unbroken up to World War 2.

In the north end of the island a match at Uig between a local team and a team from Portree on a Thursday afternoon in February 1888 heralded the revival. People from capitals, however small, tend to have a healthy conceit of themselves and it seems the Portree men expected a walk-over. But they were sorely disappointed and had to admit shamefaced defeat before the final whistle, losing by a margin of one hail to two hails and three points. (Under "Strathglass rules" single points were awarded for balls driven past the goal-line outside the goals and over the crossbar.)

At the very end of that year, on 29 December 1888, the *Oban Times* reported briefly: "A shinty club has just been formed at Bernisdale. Thirty-two members have been enrolled, and Mr MacDonald of Skeabost, who is to provide the shinties, is captain. It is expected that a match will take place before the winter is over between this new club and the Portree Shinty Club." The news must have brought joy to the heart of Mairi Mhor nan Oran, who had returned to her native home some six years earlier — her beloved *"bugha mor"* would ring again with the sound of camans!

Whether the hoped-for match with Portree took place is not on record, but the formation of the Bernisdale club is an occasion to note in the annals of Skye shinty. The crofting district at the head of Loch Snizort was to be a notable nursery of the skills of the caman, supplying Skye with some of the most glittering names ever to have graced its team lists.

Circumstances in Bernisdale were favourable for the formation of the new club. Apart from the local shinty tradition the district was a peaceful oasis in the strife-torn Skye of the 1880s; the bitterness which characterised landlord-crofter relations over much of the island was noticeably absent. Almost alone among Highland lairds Lachlan Macdonald of Skeabost took the part of the crofters in the land debate, and frequently tried to temper the more extreme excesses of his fellow landlords. When he was absent from home on business prominent Land League leaders from Portree often took over his role as chairman at local ceilidhs and social events. Lachlann Sgeathaboist, as he was known to fellow Gaels, was to be a supportive patron of the early Skye teams.

Lachlan Macdonald of Skeabost was a son of Lieutenant Charles Macdonald of Ord - the "M'Ian" of Alexander Smith's *A Summer in Skye*. Lachlan was reputed to be the richest man in the island, having founded the family fortune as an indigo planter in India where he served in the Behar Light Horse during the Indian Mutiny. His pro-crofter stance during the land agitation singled him out among Highland landlords. He opposed the use of the military in Skye, and shocked his fellow proprietors at a conference in Inverness by refusing to condemn tenants who deforced sheriff officers. Apart from his patronage of the original Bernisdale shinty club he was also an active supporter of Skye Camanachd in its early years.

No doubt there were a number of reasons for the revival. The ancient sport of camanachd was enjoying a new vogue throughout the Highlands and among the expatriate Gaelic communities in the cities of central Scotland. There was a buzz of excitement in the air, and much talk of standardising rules and setting up associations to administer the sport. And Skye, with a confidence born of holding centre stage in Highland politics for a decade and success in the land struggle, was in a mood to participate. But the years of conflict had also been divisive within the island community, and it needed the balm that communal activity like shinty, with its appeal to common loyalties, could bring to its raw wounds. In the next decade men who had lately been the most bitter of political foes were to sit round the same table with the single aim of promoting the island's fortunes on the shinty field.

And in the years until the end of the century the impetus that was to drive Skye forward into the mainstream of shinty development was to come from the little island capital, Portree.

Chapter 2

Portree to the fore

On a December Saturday in 1892 the click of camans and the shouts of spectators carried through the winter air in Portree. The local Athletic Club had arranged a Christmas Eve shinty match between the Macs and non-Macs of the village. After an hour's play the non-Macs trooped happily from the field, having drubbed their opponents by the handsome margin of 8 hails to 2. With the new year still young — on Monday 2 January 1893 — the Macs had a tight revenge by the odd hail in five.

At the time the games were probably seen by most people as simply an enjoyable contribution to the seasonal festivities, a welcome revival of an age-old tradition. But for some of the players and club officials they probably had greater significance. Their old, leather-bound account book shows a first credit entry of £10 under 1 October 1892 — an earnest of their determination to put sport in Skye on an organised footing. In contrast to the earlier sporadic revivals these matches can be seen in retrospect to mark the beginning of a continuous tradition of competitive shinty playing which has lasted a century. Three years later Portree Athletic Club was to change its name to Skye Camanachd Club and become the focus of island loyalty to an extent that no other organisation has ever achieved.

Most pictures of Portree around the turn of the century show a peaceful village, dreaming in the morning sunshine under a haze of white peat smoke. The houses are wrapped round the harbour in two tiers; beyond them, out of camera range, Wentworth Street leads on to Somerled Square, the landward limit of the village. Down by the Liosagarry estuary the fishermens' cottages straggle along the shoreline of Fisherfield and Lotts, looking across to a short street of similar cottages - most of them thatched - beside Joseph Johnston of Montrose's salmon fishing station on the Sligneach. Further out, along the unmetalled Dunvegan road, lie the Wool Mill and the small crofts of Sluggans, and, right on the edge of the Mointeach Mhor, the parish Poorhouse.

Around 1,300 people lived in this area, with several families crowded into some houses around the pier and in the closes behind Wentworth Street. Gaelic was their usual tongue, though most of them had some fluency in English, and the youngsters, influenced by fashion and an education system which taught them to despise their own language, were increasingly adopting it. The mill, fishing, a little farm work and the service industries provided the main sources of employment.

There were numerous craftsmen and tradesmen, ranging from a watchmaker and a saddler to any number of blacksmiths, carpenters, masons, painters and shoemakers; there was as numerous a range of shops — from specialists like dressmakers, tailors, fleshers and bakers, to a dozen or more small general merchants. A trades directory of the time, if such had existed, might have listed more than 60 names in these categories. Many stayed open late in the evening, exchanging as much gossip as they did trade. Four churches, as many hotels, three bank agents, a couple of law firms, a secondary school, and a court-house with a resident sheriff marked the town's pretensions to being a capital and gave it a small professional class.

The harbour and the pier were the real focus of the place. Every week there were 24 regular steamer movements — arrivals or departures — connecting daily with Raasay, Broadford, Plockton and the railhead at Strome; twice-weekly with Tarbert, Lochmaddy, and Dunvegan on the return trip; twice-weekly also north to Stornoway and back south to Glasgow; and every Friday evening there was a sailing to Gairloch and Poolewe and back. The villagers were used to being wakened by the 3am Tuesday morning rattle of the Claymore's anchor chain as she arrived from Stornoway, and the shouts of stevedores and sailors over the hiss and clatter of steam winches as she prepared to depart an hour later for Glasgow. And the boarding-houses around the pier were equally used to opening their doors to sleepy travellers at that unearthly hour.

But the sudden bustle of activity would soon die in the wake of the departing steamer, and the harbour would slow to the pace of fishing smacks under oar and sail, and the occasional coastal schooner tacking in by the Sgeir Mhor. Something of the flavour of the village in 1905 is captured by J A MacCulloch in his book, *The Misty Isle of Skye*:—

> Steamers come and go, bringing mails and cargoes; these connect the place with the outer world; carts move leisurely pierwards or countrywards to carry off these cargoes; the country-folk come in to town with their shaggy ponies bearing panniers to do their shopping; the place swarms with shops; yet at any hour of the day you may look upon the square or wander through the streets and fancy yourself in Sleepy Hollow. Business goes slowly and requires much cogitation and lengthy discussion; as leisurely goes pleasure; and though now or then some new game or sport is attacked, enthusiasm, never very strong, soon dies down and things become as they were. Yet the game of shinty is played with something approaching to enthusiasm, and if a dance is announced a real frenzy is awakened and the hoochs of the reel-dancers wake the echoes of the assembly room till dawn steals through the windows.

In 1892, however, a tingle of excitement beyond the prospect of a dance still lingered in the Portree air from the previous decade. If the front-line trenches of the land war of the 1880s were in Kilmuir and Staffin, Glendale and Braes, the information and command centre was in Portree, the most politically motivated town in the Highlands at the time. Its name was heard in the corridors of Westminster, usually with misgiving. From the local post office the telegraph messages buzzed urgently to Glendale and Kilmuir to warn of impending troop movements. Seldom were the crofters caught off guard. And when crofters were thrown in gaol the Portree merchants, to their lasting credit, were at the forefront of efforts to bail them out or succour their stricken families.

It was a time of rare fervour. The villagers gathered at the pier to hiss and boo in October 1886 as Sheriff Ivory and his entourage of police and marines landed from the warships and marched up to his headquarters in the Royal Hotel.(Some locals had other priorities. The story is told of the penniless drouth who dashed into the teeming bar when the first ship nosed round the Udarn, and announced: "The man-o'-wars is arrived!" — and stayed to gulp the discarded drams as the crowd rushed for the door!)

Six months later they gathered to give Michael Davitt, the Irish Land League leader, a tumultuous welcome as he stepped ashore from the Glencoe on his way to address an outdoor meeting of around 4,000 crofters in the magnificent natural arena of Uig. "Feeling ranged between blood heat and bursting point," according to *The Highlander*. "The distinguished Irish patriot was met by a large crowd who cheered continuously and waved banners enthusiastically. A procession was quickly formed and, preceded by two pipers and followed by a surging crowd, Mr Davitt walked to the Portree Hotel. All along the streets he was heartily cheered, tottering old men vieing to outshout demonstrative youth...." (The Portree Hotel was the rival headquarters, where the crofters' friends waited for whatever snippets of information sympathetic reporters, and indeed lawyers working for the authorities, could glean from the Royal.)

Those who were to devote their energies to Skye shinty in the next decade were in the heat of the action — on both sides. On an early November afternoon in 1886 the *cailleachs* of Sleepy Hollow peered round their doorways in utter disbelief as John Gunn Mackay, influential village merchant and radical land reformer — and a man who ranks high, perhaps the highest, among the founding fathers of Skye shinty — was marched from his shop and unceremoniously dumped in the old prison at the Meall. Following a mass meeting in the village on Monday 1 November to protest against the return of the Marines to Skye the redoubtable JG, as he was commonly known, had written to the Home Secretary describing Ivory as "a judicial monster"! That was mild for JG, but enough to have Ivory jumping up and down screaming slander and defamation. And a couple of hours later the *cailleachs* had more astounding news to whet their tongues. Norman Maclean, village carpenter and JG's henchman in Land League politics (as he was soon to be in shinty promotion), had also been tossed into the cells! The fiery Tormod Beag (Wee Norman) was alleged to have obstructed two policemen who had tried to enter the meeting to find out what was afoot.

By late evening, however, both were free, bailed out at £100 apiece by two other village tradesmen, the Kemp brothers (another name that was to grace Skye shinty in the next century). Ivory was subsequently "persuaded" by higher authority that he would be wiser not to pursue his ludicrous vendetta and the charges were dropped.

John Gunn Mackay, familiarly JG, a founding member of both Skye Camanachd and the first Glasgow Skye club, was one of the most forthright and effective of the Land League activists. He was born in 1849 in Lochalsh, where his Sutherland-born father was a schoolmaster, and brought up in Skye, his mother being from Bracadale. He learned the draper's trade in Glasgow, where he was sacked in 1881 (but subsequently reinstated) after making "an impassioned speech" at an Irish Land League rally in the city. He set up business in Portree in 1885 in the appropriately-named Gladstone Buildings on Quay Brae, and immediately became embroiled in land politics, Gaelic affairs and shinty. In the early 1890s he was a Land League councillor for Portree on the recently formed Inverness County Council but refused invitations to stand for Parliament on health grounds. On a visit to Portree in 1917 Norman Nicolson of Scorrybreck met JG and left this picture of him:—

"He was an old chap with a grey beard and a tam-o-shanter on his head, but what you noticed most and first were his fiery old eyes — I've never seen eyes like them.....The subject he was keenest on was the restoration to the crofters of the land now saved for grouse and deer. He was constantly urging Government action to resume these great empty areas from the grocers and the Yankee millionaires, and from the people he hated most of all — the rich English and those Scottish owners who had deserted their people. 'Think what it would mean to the Empire now,' he would say, 'if these empty glens were filled with the old types of crofters and their families...I've been preaching this for years and they can see it now when it's too late, and all I've got is abuse. I'm called a "Soshalist" and a "rotter" and the like o' that.' "

Norman Maclean in Volunteer uniform. Born in Diurinish in 1855 Tormod Beag had a carpenter's business in Portree and during the 1880s kept the Glendale crofters informed of planned police and troop movements against them. With JG Mackay and Myles Macinnes he was one of the pro-Irish Home Rule group of radicals known to political opponents as "the Portree clique." He is likely to have taken part in the 1886 Volunteer "mutiny" over deploying the military against crofters. Around the turn of the century he removed his business to Glasgow where his sons — and notably John, the extrovert and flamboyant "Kaid" Maclean — were deeply involved with the Glasgow Skye club. His daughter, Mary B. Maclean, was a well-known elocutionist and frequently performed on city Gaelic platforms. His grandson, Major Stewart of Skeabost Hotel, recalls Tormod Beag with affection: "When I was a child he used to pay me 3d every Saturday to brush his coat before he went out to watch Glasgow Skye play shinty. He was a very matey sort of man, he liked company and enjoyed going for a dram. But he had a forceful personality — you couldn't push him around!"

But in that same turbulent month a much more serious and potentially explosive protest took place in Portree. On Tuesday 2 November 1886, 34 members of the Skye Highland Rifle Volunteers (the part-time territorials of the time) presented their commanding officer, Colonel Alexander MacDonald of Treaslane, with their resignations to show their anger at the use of British forces against the crofters. "It is probable that the resignations will not be accepted by the officers of the corps, and it is not unlikely that a court martial will be held in a few days to deal with the leaders," the *Northern Chronicle* reported. The following week, accompanied by their womenfolk and a retinue of supporters, 20 of the volunteers emphasised their stance by marching to the Drill Hall to hand in their uniforms. Drill-Instructor Hutcheson refused to accept them; but the gesture finally provoked the authorities into action. On Tuesday 16 November Major Gordon, battalion adjutant, arrived from Inverness headquarters to present the men with an ultimatum at a private meeting; withdraw the resignations within 48 hours — or else the matter would be reported to the Secretary of State for War! In other words the threat of formal court martial, and harsh punishment for the ringleaders, was only too real. Had that happened the land war could well have exploded into active violence, but the men wisely decided that they had made their point and could achieve nothing more by further insubordination. Five of those identified as ringleaders — two sergeants and three privates — were summarily dismissed. Others retaliated by refusing to re-enlist when their time was up.

The names of those involved have never been released, but, given the close relationship between Skye shinty and the Volunteers right up to World War 1, it would be very surprising if some of the future players and officials were not among them. It would be completely in character for Tormod Beag, who was certainly a Volunteer, to be among the leaders; it's also a fair bet that Myles Macinnes, blacksmith, merchant and active Land Leaguer (with Tormod Beag and JG Mackay he formed what the rest of the Highlands knew as the "Portree clique" for their radical anti-landlord, pro-Irish stance) was near the centre of the action.

What is beyond doubt is that the commanding officer, Alexander Macdonald, suffered a tense fortnight — possibly the worst of what for him had been an anxious and troublesome decade. He was a brother of Harry Macdonald, Viewfield, whose absence in India had been blamed in 1881 for the lack of the traditional New Year game. As factor for most of Skye's large estates Alasdair Ruadh an Domhnallaich had been in the forefront of most clashes with crofters and the Land League. Apart from his busy Portree legal practice (later to become Macdonald & Fraser) and his factoring duties, he was also chairman or clerk of innumerable parochial boards and parish school boards, a bank agent, a Clerk of the Peace, as well as holding a proliferation of lesser posts — all of which led the national press to dub him "the uncrowned King of Skye"! In other words Alasdair Ruadh was immensely powerful, but hardly popular, especially among crofters. Even so, he was to prove a stout supporter of the emerging Skye shinty team, as also was his second-in-command in the Volunteers, Lachie Ross of the Royal Hotel and Glenvarigill Farm, another pillar of the establishment for whom the Land League were no better than a Fenian rabble.

Among such alarms and excursions it's surprising that the Portree people found time for organised sporting activities. That they did is due to the arrival in their midst in the spring of 1886 of Fred L Catcheside, a young lay reader

Six-footers to a man.... a colour party from the Skye Volunteers face the camera at the Meall, Portree, before setting off for a late Victorian royal review in Edinburgh.

The Portree company of the Inverness Highland Rifle Volunteers battalion was first formed in 1867 when 81 men enrolled "in a few minutes" at a meeting in the court house. A year later their establishment was fixed at one captain, two lieutenants or ensigns, one assistant-surgeon and 159 other ranks. They included 20 men from Raasay and one of the ensigns was Alexander Macdonald — *Alasdair Ruadh* — later to command the company. Their uniform was a grey doublet, Macdonald of the Isles tartan kilt and plaid, green and red hose with green tops, and a Glengarry bonnet with the Macdonald crest.

In 1881, when the territorial system was introduced, the battalion, with Portree now as 'H' company, was affiliated to the Queen's Own Cameron Highlanders but did not adopt their uniform until 1896. On 31 March 1908, under the Territorial Army scheme, the battalion ceased to exist and was reconstituted next day as the 4th Battalion Queen's Own Cameron Highlanders.

Most Skye shinty players of the time were Volunteers; payment for the annual camp and various allowances provided useful additional income. The resident drill instructor based in Portree usually helped out with team training. On New Year's Day the Volunteers normally held a shooting competition at Cnoc na Targaid near Creagliath, a practice that may have helped kill the traditional shinty match. What the shooting was like on that particular day is anyone's guess! But inter-regimental competitions were common and a number of the company, including Angus Ross (second left, above), competed at Bisley.

attached to St Columba's Episcopal Church. Being of an athletic bent and notic-
ing the lack of recreational facilities for like-minded youngsters he immediately
set about providing them — hence the formation of Portree Athletic Club, which
seems to have been a multi-sport organisation with sections devoted to football,
rugby, lawn tennis and a number of indoor activities for winter evenings. Despite
much tut-tutting around the village that a man with church connections (albeit
with a church so woefully weak on Calvinistic verities!) should be involved in pro-
fane exercises, the club seems to have prospered. And when Mr Catcheside
moved to Stornoway in March 1888 he was presented with a purse of sovereigns
in the Portree Hotel, and JG Mackay took the opportunity of noting "how much
the shinty club was indebted to him, because it was by his influence it was incor-
porated with the Athletic Club." This rather suggests that a dormant and inac-
tive shinty team had been given the kiss-of-life by Mr Catcheside's organisational
leadership.

It may also have been due to his influence that a football team from
Stornoway arrived in Portree in late November 1886 to play a 10-a-side match
against the Athletic Club. The game itself was unexceptional (Portree won 1-0)
but it provoked an interesting response. An enraged Edinburgh Highlander wrote
to the press complaining about the "degeneracy" of Skyemen and Lewismen
playing "this brutal game" to the neglect of "the manly and honest Celtic game"
of shinty. "Are there no Highlanders in Skye or the Lews who will resuscitate the
real Highland game of shinty?" he asked. As far as Skye was concerned the
answer was to be positive; and in the case of Lewis, where shinty was still played
by children in the Uig district up to World War 1, distance rather than "degeneracy" probably led to its demise. Even the much shorter crossing to the mainland
was to pose major problems for Skye.

How active the Athletic Club was on the shinty field as the 1880s gave way to
a new decade is impossible to say. Apart from the Uig debacle, there are no press
reports of matches. Perhaps that experience blunted their enthusiasm a little; or
perhaps football was too fashionable a counter-attraction (though a report of
1891 saying the football club had been "reconstituted" suggests it, too, was in
the doldrums); or perhaps village politics got in the way occasionally. While the
rest of Skye slowly returned to normality, the spirit of radicalism still glowed red
in the village. Two months before the Christmas game with which the Macs and
the non-Macs heralded the lasting revival of shinty in Skye, the Portree Land
Leaguers staged a last foray. At noon on Monday 17 October 1892 some 50 villagers, led by a piper and local merchant Donald Stewart, marched about a mile
out of the village and held a demonstration on a knoll above the old water reser-
voir on Scorrybreck Farm. Their purpose, Mr Stewart explained, was to stake out
claims for allotments for the village at Achachore and Malagan (now the east half
of Achachore), and fishermen's holdings at Beal. It was scandalous that the village children's health should suffer because they only had an inadequate supply
of Swiss tinned milk while Mr John Stewart, tacksman of Scorrybreck's 72
square miles, refused them grazing for a single cow. There were more rousing

speeches in similar vein from a number of speakers — with JG, Tormod Beag and Myles Macinnes well to the fore — before the demonstrators returned to the village to address a larger audience and demand their claim be raised at Inverness County Council.

The issue was raised again at a public meeting in January 1893, this time with the Home Farm — whose tenant was about to leave — earmarked as the site for the proposed allotments. Apart from the matter of children's health, Dr Dewar lent medical weight to the claim by saying he found it impossible to get milk for his patients. It was decided to make a direct appeal to the proprietor, Lord Macdonald. JG Mackay was typically forthright. "Lord Macdonald draws about £500 of feu duty from Portree, and there is not even a public park or a playground where the children can play without trespassing!" he said. But Lord Macdonald was not forthcoming, and the Home Farm went to a new tenant. The dispute was to return and haunt Portree Athletic Club two years later; and, indeed, almost blow it apart.

Meanwhile the club entered its 1893-94 season playing both football and shinty, its first game being a football match with teams chosen from within its own membership and its major expenditure being a sum of £1 9s 6d for footballs. But under the date 30 November 1893 a key entry appears in the account book: shinty association — 10s! Portree Athletic Club had joined the Camanachd Association, formed at a conference in Kingussie some seven weeks previously. It was a clear statement of intent to be part of the rapidly developing shinty world on the mainland; from now on football would have to take second place.

Some days earlier, on Saturday 21 November, the club had opened its shinty season, again from within its own resources, but this time — by way of variation from the previous year's Mac v non-Mac formula — the Natives played the Strangers, the latter being those resident in Skye but born outwith the island. This had the extremely satisfactory result of giving the Natives a 13-0 win. (Would that all Skye teams had followed the pattern down the last century!) Otherwise, according to the local correspondent, there was little to note apart from the fact that the wind blew down the incline of the pitch (one of the back Home Farm fields with a stiff nor'-easter, possibly?), and some good play from Myles Macinnes and the brothers Angus and William Ross in the Native forward-line. All three were to serve the team well in its early years.

But, of course, playing the variations on Macs and Natives, and whatever other combinations ingenuity might come up with, might be fine for practice but could hardly be called competitive progress. Outside competition was clearly needed, and minds must have bent to this as the club prepared for its annual dance in January 1894. By invitation only, at a cost of 9s 4d to the club for printing the cards, this was clearly a social event in the village calendar rather than a fund-raiser. There was regret that Harry Macdonald, Viewfield, "the genial chieftain of the club", could not be present (India again) but Mrs Macdonald was there to oversee the musical entertainment, and she also brought her house servants to serve the buffet. "Dancing continued with unflagging energy till far into Thursday morning" despite the fact that the refreshment room "was conducted on total abstinence principles" — or perhaps because of it?

Meanwhile, with Uig still a four-lettered word in the Portree vocabulary, eyes turned southwards in search of new and challenging fields to conquer. By some chance of fate, or possibly family relationship, they lit on Breakish, a township that seemed to have continued nurturing the New Year game tradition. So at 7am on Saturday 27 January the Portree team followed captain Malcolm Macinnes, brother of Myles, onto the mail steamer and landed at Broadford two hours later — in the face of a full-blown gale! Wisely, they decided to have breakfast in the hotel before tackling the four-mile hike to the Breakish pitch, where they arrived at 11am, numb from the horizontal rain and hail. It took a further hour for the Breakish team to muster; they had thought that nobody was foolhardy enough to venture forth in such weather — not even Portree men! The game finally started at noon with ten men a side, but without a referee and, as quickly became apparent, with two sets of rules. In fact, it was a clash between old and new; Breakish following centuries-old local tradition, while Portree had the latest update on rules from the Camanachd Association. As soon as Billy Ross slipped in Portree's opening goal from a couple of yards within five minutes of the start, the contest threatened to turn into a re-run of an ancient clan battle, as the *Inverness Courier's* correspondent noted:—

> Then arose questionings and grumblings by the Breakish team, who held that no hail could be scored by a little drive from a short distance; and the Portree team, seeing the crowd gathering into the field and getting excited, were about to give up claiming the hail, when one of the Breakish team — Hector Robertson — came up and demanded fair play, and got his men to allow the claim. Then, following the Breakish rules, ends were changed; and with the wind and incline favouring Portree, it was expected that speedy scoring would ensue. But the Portree backs fell off terribly. However, after a quarter of an hour's hard work, Ross gave a good drive, which certainly the Portree team believed to be a hail, but the claim for which they did not press keenly against the stout denial of their opponents, and so a good twenty minutes passed before an admitted hail was scored — the work being done this time by Macinnes's tipping the ball to Ross to the hail mouth, and Ross tipping it in. Then Breakish got the advantages, and after a long spell of hard work they scored their first hail amidst the great acclamations of the spectators. After this the home team warmed to their work , and showed better stuff all round than their opponents. They played their own homely game in grand form — one hand on the caman and one clearing the way — always lifting the ball when it fell into the lake that was in the middle of the field and running off with it to a corner for a free hit. At this stage in the game, after 75 minutes play, Malcolm Macinnes was seized with cramp in the leg, and amid cries of "Leave him alone" from the spectators to the gentleman who came to attend to him, the Breakish team pressed forward, and a good drive from their back was greeted with cheers from the crowd. The Portree team thought it so unjust to claim as a hail a ball that they believed to be a couple of yards wide of the post, that they retired from the field. When their Captain got his leg right and got up, he thought it as well not to resume the game.

The Breakish team were in grand form over what they claimed to be a draw, and treated their opponents to refreshments on the field. They are good stuff, and have some excellent players; but they must learn something about rules. In particular they must learn that it is no game to play behind the hailpost and tip the ball back to a friend. There was no umpire or referee. Mr James Campbell, Broadford, timed the play, an unecessary task owing to the habit of changing ends at each hail.

And so, total abstinence totally forgotten, it all seemed to end fairly amicably with a dram. Breakish were quite happy with their hard-earned "draw", while Portree were quite convinced in their own minds that they had won a 2-1 victory over the unruly mob from the south. As they cork-screwed homewards on the evening steamer their minds may already have turned to fresh challenges on the mainland; preferably against a team that knew the rules, had access to a referee, and where they might have some chance of playing till the final whistle, something they had not achieved in either of their outings in Skye! But that ambition was more than a year from fulfilment, and intervening events almost killed it completely.

The 1894-95 season began with a committee-room storm that made the gale-swept field at Breakish seem as calm as a summer rose-garden. Two years earlier, when a new tenant entered Portree Home Farm, it was understood that the field behind the Episcopal Church was to be reserved as a recreation ground for the village. On that basis the Athletic Club had spent over £30 draining and levelling it, and for a four-month period in 1893 had paid Mr Angus Campbell, the tenant in question, a total of £6 16s in rental for its use for two hours on Saturday evenings. But when they met him in October 1894 to formalise and extend the arrangement, he refused to do so, and indeed denied them the use of any of the farm parks. An appeal to Lord Macdonald's factor to intervene had so far failed to break the impasse. There was also smouldering resentment because Lord Macdonald had rejected an offer from 25 householders to lease the farm on a co-operative basis, and run it on behalf of the village. For the previous three weeks Portree had been seething with the rumour that the next shinty meeting was likely to be an explosive one. Given the volatile personalities involved, and the strong political convictions of some of them, it is little wonder that angry passions were released when the Athletic Club committee met on Friday 9 November.

Norman Maclean, who needed less than an excuse to slate the landlords, opened the hostilities. He was all for marching to the park next day "with flags and banners flying" and sealing their claim to it with a game of shinty. Colonel Alexander Macdonald, the club president (his military style came from the Volunteers), and every bit as fiery as Norman, angrily decried such illegal tactics, and threatened to resign if any such attempt was made. Members quickly polarised as it became clear that Tormod Beag and Alasdair Ruadh were quite ready to revive the land war. It's probable that most were in sympathy with Norman, but opinion swung the other way when JG Mackay — normally clamouring for direct action — warned of the danger of irreparably splitting the club, and suggested a deputation should lobby Lord Macdonald personally. Major Lachie Ross (again a Volunteer title), now retired to Glenvarigill Farm, tried to ease the tension by offering the free use of a field, as also did Mr Maclaren, his manager in the Royal Hotel. Though both fields were a distance from town the offer was finally accepted as an interim measure after hours of heated debate. Meanwhile pressure was to be brought on Lord Macdonald as landlord to persuade Mr Campbell to release the park. On the Saturday of the following week two nine-a-side teams chosen by Colonel Macdonald and Major Ross met,

Harry Macdonald, Viewfield, (right of main picture) and brother John at Redcliff with the Lodge (now the Coolin Hills Hotel) in the background. They were sons of Harry Macdonald, solicitor and bank agent in Portree, and both patrons of Skye Camanachd. Harry (1855 - 1905) was club chieftain, took an active interest in the running of the club, and sometimes travelled to mainland ties. He was keen on sport and one of the founders of the Skye Gathering games. He spent 12 years as an indigo planter in India and frequently returned there on business. The memorable and much-loved Colonel "Jock" Macdonald was his son.

Inset is a portrait of Colonel Alexander Macdonald of Treaslane, as he was known to the Volunteers — *Alasdair Ruadh an Domhnallaich* (Red Alex Macdonald) to most Skye crofters who had little love for him. Alasdair (1840-1899) was a brother of Harry and John Macdonald but, unlike them, a contentious and controversial figure. He followed his father in the legal practice in Portree. The historian I M M MacPhail has written of him: "As a lawyer, Macdonald felt bound by the legal system prevailing, harsh though it was and as he knew it to be." Despite the hatred for him on the estates which he factored, the 20 or so crofters on his own small estate of Treaslane enjoyed some of the smallest rents in Skye, and held him in respect. Whatever else, he was an ardent supporter of the emerging shinty club.

probably at Glenvarigill, to open the season. Since it was really a dressed-up practice match the fact that Colonel Macdonald's team emerged 6-3 victors hardly matters. And yet, in a sense, it was probably the most important game the club ever played; it was evidence that the warring political factions were willing to sink their differences long enough to make common cause for the good of Skye shinty. A week earlier few would have predicted the match would take place.

During the winter months presumably some gentle back-door diplomacy was taking place between club, landlord and farmer to try to solve the dispute. But feelers were out in other directions as well — towards Beauly, in fact. The result was that Beauly Shinty Club, also founded in 1892, invited Portree Athletic to a friendly challenge match, their first test of skill against mainland competition. Why Beauly? Part of the answer may be that members of the two teams already knew each other through the annual training camps of the 1st Volunteer Battalion Cameron Highlanders where, as "small townies", they tended to make common cause against the massed ranks from Inverness (and also looked down their noses at their country cousins!). But more substantially, two members of the Portree team — Dr D D Macdonald, who ran a chemist's shop in Portree, and Kenneth Macrae, the sheriff clerk — belonged to Beauly, and were in a position to smooth the way. We can be sure the challenge was not taken lightly, and over the winter, though no shinty activity is recorded, practice matches must have taken place. The cash book records the purchase of two shinty balls, at 2s and 3s, possibly from a local cobbler; and 18 shinty sticks at £2 14s (3s each), freight 1s 6d, almost certainly from Inverness. Under the latest Camanachd Association rules there would be 16 players in each team.

And so on the morning of Wednesday 6 March 1895 the 16 "braw lads" of Portree (as the *Inverness Courier* dubbed them), accompanied by Lawrence Skene, club vice-president, boarded the steamer, sailed past unruly Breakish, and arrived at Strome in time for the eastbound 11am train. The great adventure had begun. They arrived in Beauly just after 2pm and were immediately whipped off to the Lovat Arms Hotel for "a substantial luncheon"; then just time for an official photograph in the hotel grounds by Mr MacMahon from Inverness before arriving at the ground, a nearby farm field, for a 3.30pm throw-up. Unfortunately the surface consisted of a few inches of sodden, newly-thawed soil on a still-frozen base. But at least there was a sense of occasion. Business had practically come to a halt in Beauly, and the crowd who stood almost ankle-deep in the touchline mud was estimated at "several hundreds, and included a large proportion of the fair sex."

The game itself was hardly a classic, understandable on a slow and watery surface with the ball frequently embedded in the mud. The superior build of the Skyemen impressed some of the spectators, but Beauly — according to the *Courier* — was quickly to establish an almost monotonous command of the game. Only the efforts of D Macpherson in the Portree goal, and his backs, D Michie, Myles Macinnes and Kenny Macrae, prevented an early score:—

Time after time shots were driven into the goal mouth and at length,after about twenty minutes of one-sided play, the ball was popped through by Maclean from a fine pass by Tom Fraser. The hail was proclaimed with cheers by the spectators, who, in their anxiety, trespassed within the flags, and the Beauly men, encouraged with success, renewed the attack....Portree, however, showed no intention of taking their defeat lying down. They pulled themselves together, and, time after time, resisted the dashing charges of the Beauly forwards ....It was a trying time for the Portree half-backs and backs, and they did not receive the support from their forwards that they had a right to expect. Some of the forwards, notably the captain (Angus Ross) and Dr Macdonald, put in a great deal of hard work, but the front line as a whole, did not exhibit the dash and combination which tell so much more effectively than individual efforts, however well judged.

But at least Portree had held the score to 1-0 at half-time. And they began the second half with such spirited attacks that for a short while it seemed that fortunes might change until the game settled back into the familiar pattern, and Beauly got the ball in the net four times, one of which was disallowed. At the final whistle the score was 4-0, and Portree were well beaten but by no means disgraced:—

Though fairly broken down towards the finish, the Portree team fought the losing battle to the end. It could not be denied, and it was no disgrace for a team playing its first match, that they were fairly beaten by superior speed, combination, and command of club and ball. Still, the result is not, perhaps, a perfect indication of the comparative merits of the teams. The long journey from Portree to Beauly might have deprived the Skyemen of some of their pristine dash and staying power.

And the *Ross-shire Journal's* man-on-the-spot was much in agreement with his *Courier* colleague:—

It was not long until the home team showed their superiority and agility over their opponents in playing a more scientific and combined game. The strangers wrought hard and exerted themselves to the utmost but it was no use, the odds of smartness and tact were against them.

It was then back to the Lovat Arms where the team sat down with their hosts to "a very satisfying repast". There followed a succession of hearty and lengthy speeches, full of Victorian hyperbole, in which club officials paid fulsome compliments to their opponents. Innumerable toasts were drunk before "Auld Lang Syne" brought the official part of the evening to a close. There may well have been sore heads on next day's long journey home, but few sore hearts; despite defeat the venture had been well worth while and a pointer for things to come. Only the club treasurer may have had a few doubts. A two-day mainland trip to Beauly cost £15 15s 6d in team expenses against £2 for the trip to Breakish, and club finances had hitherto been geared to the latter.

As the season ended the team were left with one rather curious duty to perform. The club had decided "to extend a compliment" to Harry Macdonald of Viewfield, their chieftain, on his being elected a member of the Parish Council during his absence in London. They chose to do so as he and Lawrence Skene left an election meeting in support of Mr James Baillie, the Unionist candidate

Any unseemly tendency to brag about the superiority of islanders should be quelled by the first team Skye sent to the mainland, still under the name of Portree Athletic. It owed a lot to the eastern Highlands. Both Kenny Macrae, who gave a lifetime of loyal service to Skye Camanachd as player and official, and Dr Macdonald were Beauly men. John Cameron, governor of Portree poorhouse, was from Dingwall and son Hector was born in Kilmorack. John Melville's father, a local policeman, hailed from Brora. Duncan Michie was also a mainlander, possibly from Ross-shire. The rest, so far as is known, lined up for the "natives" in the informal matches of the day. Myles Macinnes, powerful as blacksmith and politician, was originally from Sleat. The Ross brothers, Billy a cobbler and Angus a postal clerk, had Portree and Strath loyalties. Calum Macneil had Glenmore connections. John Grant, John Macdonald who was later pier agent, and George Mackenzie the local road surveyor's son, were all of Skye stock, as almost certainly were R Mackinnon, C Macdougall and D Macpherson. And though mill owner Lawrence Skene took his paternal name from Aberdeenshire a generation earlier, his maternal side was Skye. They were, in fact, typical of Portree as a village community — a mixture of local crofting stock and incoming officials and tradesmen whose children were brought up there, some to contribute permanently to its life, others to move on. They could toss words like "native" and "incomer" around as banter for they belonged to a common culture; most appear in the 1891 census and claim to speak both Gaelic and English. They set the still enduring seal on Skye Camanachd's heavily Gaelic identity, an identity which was to be reinforced when the direct input of talent from the crofting districts began to swell early this century. Pictured at Beauly are: Back row, left to right, John Grant, C Macdougall, R Mackinnon; Centre, D E Macpherson, Myles Macinnes, Hector Cameron, John Cameron, John Macdonald, Duncan Michie, Ken Macrae; Front, Dr D D Macdonald, Angus Ross, Geo W Mackenzie (secretary), William Ross (captain), Calum Macneil, John Melville, Lawrence J Skene (referee).

in the forthcoming general election. They unhitched the horses from his carriage and, with a piper leading, team members pulled it with its two passengers the full mile to Viewfield. There they presented their chieftain with the team photograph from their Beauly expedition.

All in all it seems rather a bizarre and, indeed, servile performance for an organisation containing a fair proportion of members publicly professing radical principles. But perhaps there was more to it than meets the eye.Certainly, in a brief speech Angus Ross, the club captain, took the opportunity of reminding Messrs Macdonald and Skene that "a felt want in the village is a park for practice", and with both of them now parish councillors he hoped they would exert themselves in that direction. Obviously the Home Farm affair was still unresolved and still rankled.

It may well be that the summer saw some more quiet diplomacy exercised over the issue. In any case, at the club's annual general meeting on 11 October 1895 Kenneth Macrae announced from the chair that "Mr Campbell, Home Farm, had kindly agreed to grant the club the use of a park to play in". And, much more momentously and significantly, the members of Portree Athletic Club decided unanimously they would have a new name - Skye Camanachd!

Chapter 3

Onward to the Cup

The choice of Skye Camanachd as the new name had a number of implications. It meant that the club would concern itself solely with shinty, leaving the other sports which the old Athletic Club had dabbled in from time to time to fend for themselves. It also proclaimed that the club represented the whole of the island rather than just the village of Portree. This was to give it access to a much larger pool of playing skills, evidenced by the contribution made by the districts of Braes and Bernisdale down the years. But the transformation did not happen overnight. While the telegraph, fast steamers and trains gave Skye relatively easy access to the mainland and the south, internal communications still moved at the pace of the horse and trap and the mail coach. Portree was a four-and-a-half hour coach journey from Dunvegan, and the Staffin seamen thought nothing of a 20 mile overnight walk by a moorland track, with a heavy sea-chest on their shoulders, to catch the morning steamer. In such circumstances it was virtually impossible to gather players from a wide area for regular practice. So a tendency to rely on players resident around Portree continued until motor transport revolutionised communications in the new century.

The impetus for change came from events outwith the island. While the Beauly trip must have whetted the players' desire to be part of the wider world of shinty, exciting moves within the Camanachd Association demanded a response. At its annual meeting in September 1895 Lord Lovat, the president, proposed that a trophy be put up for immediate competition during the forthcoming season; the Camanachd Cup was born. Kenneth Macrae had been present at this meeting and was able to report its future plans for shinty to the club's annual meeting. The decision to change the name, indicating a determination to participate fully in the new developments, was the club's answer.

The new name, with its larger constituency, was reflected in the new committee. While Harry Macdonald, Viewfield, remained chieftain, and many of the members of the old Portree club provided the core of the committee, new names like Lachlan Macdonald of Skeabost, one of the founders of the Bernisdale club, appeared on it. Some of the patrons, such as MacLeod of MacLeod or R M Livingston-MacDonald of Flodigarry, a descendant of the famous Flora Mac-Donald of the '45, may have had no previously obvious enthusiasm for shinty, but they must have been thought willing to fulfil one of the main functions of a patron — the provision of a significant financial input! For many years Skye Camanachd was to be dependent largely on the annual guinea or pound donations from its expanding list of honorary office-bearers — expanding, no doubt,

				Season	
1895					
Oct 1	To Balance			9	16
	To Lachlan Macdonald, Skeabost			1	
	To J. E. B. Baillie, M.P.			2	2
	To Capt. Willoughby, Lodge			1	
	To James Ross, Broadford			1	
	To R. R. M'Leod, Greshornish			1	1
	To Col. Macdonald, Portree			1	1
	To R. L. Macdonald, Skirinish			1	
	To D. Macdonald, Edinbane			1	
	To Macleod of M'Leod, Dunvegan			1	
	To R. L. Livingston Macdonald			1	1
	To A. D. Mackinnon, Portree				10
	To George Dickson, Do.				5
	To L. J. Skene, Do.				5
	To Proceeds of Dance			4	5
	To Received for Shinties				14
	To Ronald Macdonald, Portree				10
	To James Simpson				5
	To J. G. Mackay			1	
	To Interest on Bank Account				3 6
	To Membership entry money				2 4
1897	To Proceeds of Concert			9	
Jan	To Do. Dance			8	7 6
	To Interest on Bank %				9 4
	To Membership entry money			1	6
				49	19 10

Income for season 1895-96, starting with a credit balance of £9 16s and ending with a late entry in January 1897 to balance the books. The MP for Inverness-shire, J E B Baillie, heads the generosity stakes, followed by the local lairds with their guineas and pounds. The Portree merchants and lawyers come in at five to ten shillings (though JG Mackay is not to be outdone by any laird!) and the social events have clearly been successful. Ordinary membership at the time was a shilling.

for that very reason. Having elected its office-bearers, and generally geared itself for a new and challenging situation, Skye began its preparations for its (and, indeed, everyone else's) first season of formal competition in a time-honoured way — with a game between teams chosen by the captain and vice-captain of the club.

But their enthusiasm was suddenly dampened, though fortunately not dowsed, by a ruling from the Camanachd Association. At a meeting in November to finalise arrangements for the competition, it was unanimously agreed — without warning and in the absence of an island delegate — that Skye should be required to play all home games on the mainland, on a field provided by the Association! It had suddenly dawned on the members that, despite organising the early stages of the competition on a regional basis — with northern, central, western and southern districts — to minimise travelling expenses, the long rail and sea journey to Skye, isolated on the far fringe of the northern district, would prove a considerable burden to their clubs. And this was to prove particularly true of other clubs in the northern district, like Beauly, Caberfeidh and Lovat, clustered in a neat little economic group on the east coast. In fact it was Lord Lovat who initiated the move by dismissing a visit to Skye as "a three day's job" which most clubs would find it impossible to find time for.

Skye's reaction was immediate and spirited. Kenneth Macrae wrote to the Association that games between mainland teams might also involve three days (using Glasgow and London as an extreme example), and would frequently need two days, so why was Skye thus singled out? Lord Lovat had clearly forgotten that a mainland match for Skye was also a "three days' job" he suggested sarcastically. "There is neither law nor equity to justify the decision of the Association..... a veritable grievance exists, and the sooner it is removed the better in the interests of good feeling and fair play," he concluded.

And of course a veritable grievance did exist, though Kenneth Macrae might have been slightly over the top in asserting that a mainland match needed three days for Skye. The transport system — the early-morning departure and evening return of the Portree steamer — meant Skye could manage a mainland trip in two days. They had already demonstrated this at Beauly by playing on the day of arrival, and were to do so frequently in the future, though they may not have been in top form after a tiring and often stormy journey. But clearly the ruling placed them at an unfair disadvantage, and not only in terms of having to bear an undue share of travelling expenses. Having to devote three or two days, or even one whole day, to a match must inevitably restrict the pool of players to those who could afford the time from work, rather than to the best available. And while this was to some degree true of all teams with distant away games, Skye alone was to be denied the chance of compensating home games. Their vehement protest gained them an element of compromise. In that first Camanachd Cup draw they were awarded a bye in the first round, and drawn away against the winner of the Caberfeidh v Beauly match in the second round; it was agreed, however, that the tie should be played at Strathcarron, effectively a day's return journey for both teams.

And so, on Friday 14 February 1896, Skye took the morning steamer to Strome and a short train trip to Strathcarron to play their first truly competitive game of shinty. Their opponents, for the second time within a year, were Beauly, who had ousted Caberfeidh after a replay. How many of the previous year's team were among the 12 Skyemen who lined up at Strome is impossible to say since the only brief match report extant omits the teams. The probability is that most, if not all, of the players on the field had already faced each other, which gave neither side any particular advantage. But, even from the *Inverness Courier's* rather bald report, Beauly clearly had the edge in skill:—

> The match created no little interest, and the game was vigorously contested. At the outset the Portree men, bent on scoring, made a commendable effort, but Nicolson, the Beauly hailkeeper, cleverly averted the danger. Beauly, warming to their work, eluded the opposition, and before the call of half-time scored five hails. The closing period was a more evenly contested affair. Portree, by dint of determined play, repeatedly assailed their antagonist's fortress, and were able to score two hails. Beauly replied with another hail, and the tie resulted in a win for the Beauly by six hails to two.

At least Skye's second half performance had gone some way to redeem the flood of goals that had overwhelmed them in the first half, though it was obviously too much to hope they could recover such a lead against a superior side.

On Saturday 28 November 1896 Skye returned to Strathcarron to meet Lovat in the first round of the 1896-97 Camanachd Cup competition. It was a brilliantly sunny winter's day, with a cold wind from the hills, but this did not prevent a considerable turn-out of spectators. The islanders would not have been short of support against the eastern invaders in this area of Wester Ross with which they had many traditional connections. Harry Macdonald, the chieftain, and Lawrence Skene, vice-president, accompanied the team, which read:— Myles Macinnes; William Ross and Angus Ross; Kenneth Macrae, John Macdonald and Angus Macleod; D MacCowan, A Murchison, G H Mackay, Dr D D Macdonald, D Michie and H Cameron. Seven of them were veterans of the first challenge match with Beauly, and probably of the first Cup match as well; the newcomers were Angus Macleod; D MacCowan, Camustianavaig; Alec Murchison, of the Caledonian Hotel, Portree; and G H Mackay and D Michie, both incomers to the island.

From the throw-up Dr Macdonald and Michie got possession and raced down on the Lovat gaol, only to be repulsed by a strong defence which quickly transferred the action to the Skye goal. Here "a desperate fight occurred and the ball was '*burached*' about for a time" before Lovat slipped it in the net. For the rest of the half some stout defensive work by the Ross brothers and Macrae managed to contain constant Lovat pressure, relieved by sporadic Skye attacks which failed through poor finishing. Starting the second half with the wind behind them Skye again launched a series of attacks, one of which sent the ball past inches outside the post. But shortly afterwards they were "chagrined to see another goal registered against them, as a lovely shot from almost the centre of the field, beautifully stroked by Malcolm Fraser, evaded the eye of Macinnes, and landed in the net." From then on Lovat "not only repelled the repeated onslaughts of their opponents, but took occasion to give a very excellent and effective exhibition of the game." In the closing minutes Fraser slipped another goal past Macinnes to make the final score 3-0.

Another defeat, but again — as the *Inverness Courier* pointed out — no disgrace:—

> They fought with tenacity and pluck, which showed that they possessed the true grit necesssary in the game. Their method of play, however, was somewhat deficient in tactics. The players were anxious to leave their places, and ran all over the field. In hitting, too, they were much below their opponents, while their attempts at shooting were feeble in the extreme. These weaknesses can easily be remedied, and we should imagine that, with more practice and efforts at combination, the Portree team would be enabled by their excellent physique and stamina to hold their own against any.

And the *Northern Chronicle's* correspondent made a similar point:—

> The Skyemen play on old fashioned lines — hit and rush — and were frequently nonplussed by the fine system of passing the ball practised by the Lovat team. There is, however, splendid material in their ranks, and a few brushes, such as that of Saturday, with mainland clubs should have very beneficial results.

It may well have been that the homeward bound Skyemen, having recovered from their initial disappointment, were in full agreement with that assessment. Mainland clubs that were ousted from the Cup kept interest alive through challenge matches with neighbouring teams, with local rivalry adding a competitive edge. But that option simply wasn't open to Skye in its west coast isolation, and club finances were hard-pressed to meet competition expenses without the added burden of challenge matches in the eastern Highlands. Within the island, while the game may have been played occasionally and locally in places like Breakish and Bernisdale, there was as yet no organised competition. In any case island shinty would tend to follow the traditional style, rather than the tactical game that was developing so rapidly on the mainland. For the remainder of the season the club had little to occupy it apart from occasional practices, which would attract support only when the prospect of a competitive game supplied an incentive. But the break-through was nearer than the team could reasonably have expected. It was helped by the introduction in the 1897-98 season of the MacTavish Cup competition for northern clubs; this meant the club could look forward to at least two competitive matches in a season. Determination and a bit of luck did the rest.

The new season opened on Friday 26 November 1897 with a first round Camanachd Cup tie against Caberfeidh. It took place at Attadale, near Strathcarron, and, as so often happened with games in this area, it received minimal attention from the press. But the short report that remains speaks of a close and exciting match played in fine weather, with Skye opening with "great dash" (a much-favoured word with early shinty reporters) and scoring an early goal. Fortunately, their "dash" did not evaporate and they led 2-0 at half-time. Caberfeidh then began "to show true playing form" and scored three goals in succession, only to have Skye snatch the equaliser in a last-minute rally. A 3-3 draw against such opposition was no mean achievement, and the Skye players must have felt that, in their third competitive game, they had at last made their mark.

Certainly the mainland press were of that opinion, and the *Ross-shire Journal* sent a staff reporter to Strathcarron on the Saturday of the following week to monitor the fortunes of the local team in the replay against the islanders. "Strathpeffer v Portree: An Exciting Tussle" was the resulting headline, reflecting both the run of the game and the press's rather irritating habit of naming teams after their home towns, whatever their formal titles. Skye had five changes from their 1896 line-up, the new faces being incomer Willoughby Dunn, a clerk in the local factor's office; Willie Robertson and Murdo Ferguson (Murchadh a' chlachair), both Portree; and A Campbell and A Mackenzie, probably Portree as well though identification is uncertain. Myles Macinnes, 40-year-old veteran of the early Portree Athletic teams, had retired and Angus Ross was the goalkeeper.

The game began with "unstinted eagerness" and fast end-to-end play from both teams. Caberfeidh, after several near misses, scored in the tenth minute, but a long pass from half-back Robertson allowed the Skye forwards to equalise with "a bounding rush". A second goal from Caberfeidh was also quickly countered by Skye, and at the interval the score stood at 2-2. After "a refreshing cup of tea on the field" Skye had the ball in the net five minutes after the re-start, only to have Caberfeidh equalise a few minutes later.

> The Portree men now began to show signs of flagging and carelessness in shooting, while the "Caber" lads more than maintained the essentials that are necessary for the exhibition of good play. James Mackenzie scored the fourth hail for Strathpeffer, and after this the game might be said to be one-sided and all in favour of the "Cabers." In fact the opposition became terribly weak, and before time was called a fifth hail was registered by James Mackenzie and a sixth by Murdo Mackenzie......It was admitted on all hands that the best team won; they coalesced and leagued together in a more superior way. For the Portree, W J Robertson, William Ross, Kenneth Macrae, A Mackenzie, A Campbell and M Ferguson did yeoman service.

Even if their interest in the Camanachd competition was over for another year Skye at least had the satisfaction of having pushed their opponents to two hard-fought games, and they still had the new MacTavish Cup competition to look forward to. The winter was spent in practice and preparation. A new stock of shinties was purchased from D McPherson, Inverness, and the account book notes that a dozen of them were passed on to the "Junior Athletic Club"; obviously a policy of fostering the next generation of players was in progress. A dance, and later a concert, to replenish their dwindling coffers — the two Caberfeidh games had cost £14 6s 3d — raised £14 1s 9d. The patrons were assiduously canvassed to make sure the guinea donations kept flowing in. And then the MacTavish draw brought them a bonus — their first tie was to be with Caberfeidh, a team whose style they now knew and whom they had already held to a draw! The prospect of revenge was sweet.

The teams lined up at Strathcarron at 12 noon on Saturday 25 March 1898, a fortnight behind schedule because of stormy weather. Angus Ross was absent and his place in the Skye goal was taken by William Maclean; two new faces appeared in the outfield — John Mackinnon, Glenmore, at half-back and young Norrie Robertson, just 16, playing in the forward line alongside his brother Willie, just two years older. "A game of no little keenness was anticipated," according to the *Inverness Courier*," and anticipations were not disappointed." From the opening whistle the pace was fast, with the ball "sent spinning from goal to goal" and both sides missing the target by inches several times in the first half hour. Then a long drive from near the centre line opened the scoring for Caberfeidh.

> This reverse nettled the Portree team, and by dint of neat passing on the part of their forwards, who were playing in grand form, they very soon were able to equalise matters. The ball is again brought into play, and in less time than it takes to tell it is again netted by the Portree boys.

Skye managed to retain their 2-1 interval lead for much of the second half, helped by some wild shooting from the usually deadly Caberfeidh forwards. But they did eventually get an equaliser, whereupon "the game rages fiercer and faster than ever." Skye then got a third goal and, with their defence "impregnable against all assaults", held on to that lead to the end. All in all, the *Courier* thought it a fine sporting contest: "It may be mentioned that during the whole game the referee had no occasion to give a penalty for foul play, which is creditable to both teams."

Clearly the "few brushes" with mainland teams — six in all hitherto — which the *Northern Chronicle* reporter had recommended as a curative for hit-and-rush tactics, had begun to pay off, especially for the Skye forwards. It must have been an extremely happy team that boarded the train for Kyle (which had replaced Strome as railhead the previous year), and the onward voyage to Portree. Perhaps a forgiving toast was even drunk to Breakish in the passing! The news of their victory had travelled ahead (conveyed by telegraph to an anxious village) and a large crowd was on the pier to greet them; "the victorious team were enthusiastically cheered on their arrival, while a number of the more enthusiastic youths lighted a huge bonfire on a hill overlooking the quay in honour of the victory." All that needed doing now to book a place against Inverness in the final, was to beat Lovat in the semi-final.

On Saturday 9 April Skye were back at the now familiar field at New Kelso farm, Strathcarron. Fortunately Mr Reid, the farmer, was a shinty enthusiast who plied the teams with half-time cups of tea, provided generous post-match lunches, and tried to keep the field as playable as an ordinary stretch of agricultural turf could be kept. On this particular Saturday that wasn't too good; it had rained heavily all the previous day and there were still heavy showers, so the ground was sodden. Lovat were without two key players, including their "crack forward" Angus Maclean, who was always worth a couple of goals according to the touch-line pundits. Skye were much the heavier team and had Angus Ross back in goal, while William Maclean had moved to the left wing; all the players had appeared in recent matches. For the first quarter of an hour Lovat had most of the pressure but failed to score; then Skye broke into an attack that allowed Dunn to score.

> During the further part of the first half the play was of a very one-sided nature, the Skyemen throughout pressing, and managing to go over to the second half with a lead of four hails to nil. In the second half the Lovat men made some changes in their formation...and it was at once apparent it was a change for the better. Time and again the Skye goalkeeper was called upon to save shots from the forward trio, and eventually Michael, getting a well directed pass, secured the first goal for Lovat.

And that was about it — obviously, from the *Courier's* report, not the greatest of games, but from Skye's point of view a very satisfactory performance. No doubt the telegraph wires to Portree were humming as soon as the final whistle blew, and no doubt the pierhead crowds would be there in the evening, even if it wasn't quite bonfire weather.

Doubtless also the click of camans was to be heard throughout the village of an evening for the next fortnight as the team prepared for the big day.

In Inverness, Cup Final day, Saturday 23 April, dawned wet and stayed wet. In Portree the team trooped down to the pier to catch the 7am steamer. On arrival in Inverness around 2.30pm they were immediately whisked to the Haugh Park with no time to recover from their journey. The grass on the field was long and slippery, making running and striking difficult — "not very suitable for a fine exposition of shinty," as the *Courier* remarked. The incessant rain meant a fairly small attendance, though "a few enthusiastic Skyemen accompanied their team, and cheered them on to victory." All of them had played in one or more of the earlier games; there were two schoolboys in the side, one being Farquhar Stewart and the other Norrie Robertson.

Within minutes of the start of the game Dunn opened the scoring for Skye. This success inspired a series of attacks on the Inverness goal but with no reward, and play switched to the other end. After a period of sustained pressure the Inverness full forward got the equaliser, and indeed more might have come were it not for some very poor finishing. Neither team at this stage was playing brilliant shinty, hardly surprising in such weather and on such a pitch. But of the two there was no doubt that Skye "were showing the greater vigour and dash."

A second goal was scored by K Macrae with a well taken shot. The play livened a bit, and vigorous shinty was shown. Still the Skyemen were the oppressors and had a third goal .... and a fourth before the call of half-time, Dunn doing the needful. It is unnecessary to dilate at any length on the play in the second period. Flushed with their success the islanders demonstrated that they were ahead of their opponents. Repeatedly they formed the attacking party, and Dunn, lithe and active, never failed to send the ball home. They scored three goals in the second period.....The hardy Skyemen, whose play seemed to be an unknown quantity to the clubs on the mainland, during the course of their career surprised every club they met, and on Saturday they finished by creating not only a surprise but almost a record score.

The final score was 7-2, Inverness having got a late goal. The rest of the evening is not recorded but presumably post-match hospitality had been arranged, to be followed no doubt by less formal celebrations with some of the their friends and supporters in Inverness. What is on record is their triumphant return to Portree on Monday evening's steamer.

The town was decorated with flags, while the Skye detachment of the Cameron Volunteers saluted them with ten volleys. Upon the landing of the team, the trophy, which is a large and handsome silver cup, was carried through the village amidst enthusiastic cheering, the band of the Cameron Volunteers stepping out in front.

The squad that brought home the MacTavish Cup in 1898, with the two schoolboys, Farquhar Stewart and Norrie Robertson, seated in front. Back row: A Macleod, A M Murchison, K Macrae (Captain), W Ross, A Mackenzie, M Ferguson, Front: J J Mackay (Hon President), J Mackinnon, W M Dunn, A Ross, W J Robertson, L J Skene (Hon President)

Presumably it was not an evening for abstinence; rather an evening for letting the hair down. The late Colonel Jock Macdonald used to recount a boyhood memory of Billy Ross — who, with team captain Kenneth Macrae, had played in every game since the Beauly challenge match — unravelling his impressively waxed moustache and tying the ends behind his head! Far-fetched, perhaps, but then it had been a season for the unlikely and the improbable. In three years and seven competitive matches the "hit-and-rush" merchants from the remote western outpost of shinty had been transformed into cup heroes.

Skye Teams, 1896-98

28/11/96 (v Lovat, Camanachd Cup)

Goal, Myles Macinnes; backs, William Ross and Angus Ross; halves, K Macrae, John Macdonald and Angus Macleod; forwards, D M'Cowan, A Murchison, G H Mackay, Dr D D Macdonald, D Michie and H Cameron.

04/12/97 (v Caberfeidh, Camanachd Cup)

Goal, Angus Ross; backs, William Ross and A Murchison; half-backs, W J Robertson, M Ferguson and Angus Macleod; forwards, Kenneth Macrae (capt), G H Mackay, W M Dunn, A Campbell, A Mackenzie and H Cameron.

25/03/98 (v Caberfeidh, MacTavish Cup)

Goal, W Maclean; backs, A M Murchison and Angus Macleod; half-backs, W Ross, M Ferguson, John Mackinnon and Alex Mackenzie; forwards, K Macrae, G H Mackay, W M Dunn, Norrie Robertson and W J Robertson.

09/04/98 (v Lovat, MacTavish Cup)

Goal, A Ross; backs, A Murchison and A Macleod; half-backs, W Ross, A Mackenzie, M Ferguson and W J Robertson; forwards, K Macrae (capt) W M Dunn, G H Mackay, Norrie Robertson and William Maclean

23/04/98 (v Inverness, MacTavish Cup Final)

Goal, Angus Ross; backs, A Murchison and A Macleod; halves, W J Robertson, John Mackinnon, A Mackenzie, M Ferguson; forwards, Ken Macrae, W Ross, W M Dunn, N Robertson and F Stewart.

Chapter 4

Storms and controversy

As the new season started Skye were at last offered parity with all the other clubs; they were to be allowed to play their home games at home. Their long campaign to convince the Camanachd Association of the unfairness of their treatment, no doubt helped by their performance in the MacTavish competition, had paid off. Unfortunately, it was not to last; island weather and mainland aversion to island steamers saw to that.

Foyers was the first mainland team to try a three-day-jobbing trip westwards. They arrived in Portree in the middle of a snow-storm on the evening of Monday 28 November 1898 to try their luck in the first round of the Camanachd Cup next day. They awoke to find the pitch under seven inches of snow. Nothing daunted, Skye hired a local contractor (Mr A Cameron, at a cost of 8s) to roll the playing area, thus providing an ice-rink for the first half of the game and a churned-up quagmire for the second! And then, with "sustained dash and energy", they proceeded to thrash their visitors 5-1. Four of the Skye goals came in the first half, with each team scoring only one in the second as fatigue set in and the "dash" was dissipated in the slush. Foyers, to their credit, made no complaint; having travelled so far they had little choice but to play whatever the weather.

But Beauly, drawn away to Skye in the second round of the competition, were to prove a different matter. The east coast team were riding high at the time — none higher in Scotland in fact. For two successive years they had won the Camanachd Cup and in the summer of 1897 had travelled to London to star at the London Highland Athletic Club's annual gathering. But a visit to Skye for a clash of champions with the holders of the MacTavish Cup clearly held all the attraction of a trip to Outer Siberia without a return ticket. At first Beauly tried to arrange the game for the Christmas Day holiday, hoping to charter a special train to Kyle and a steamer to Portree, but no steamer was available. Then they appealed to Skye to play on the mainland, but the islanders resolutely refused to give up their home advantage. Finally the game was played at Portree on Tuesday 27 December 1898 with Beauly girning that they would have to play "several second-rate players, as several of the team cannot get away for three days at a time", exactly the point that Skye had been making for three seasons. And against this querulous background the Skye weather gods decided to take a hand in favour of their home team — although perhaps they overdid it a bit!

Match day dawned to a driving gale, with frequent showers of rain and sleet. With the gale behind them Beauly managed to establish a 4-0 lead by half-time. In the second half the weather worsened, and one of the goals was blown down and swayed erratically for the rest of the match. Despite the conditions Beauly scored another goal, while Skye managed to get two in return, and then, half-way through the second half, scored a third which was hotly disputed by Beauly but awarded by the referee, G H Mackay, who had played for Skye for the previous two seasons. There are conflicting stories of what happened next but the referee's version in his subsequent report to the Camanachd Association reads:—

> I carried the ball thereafter up to midfield and blew my whistle, but, on looking round, I observed the Beauly men were leaving the field, and that without assigning to me any reason for their conduct. The Portree team were on the field and ready to play, and the captain, seeing that the opposing team had left the ground, formally claimed the tie which, in the circumstances, I awarded in favour of Portree.

The Beauly team, however, were adamant that they had appealed to the referee to abandon the game, and that he had agreed to do so because of the severity of the weather, although he had then changed his mind under pressure from the local team. At an angry protest meeting in Beauly after the team's return the unfortunate G H Mackay was berated as being "quite unfit to discharge effectively the duties of referee", and it was alleged he had consulted spectators before making decisions. A formal protest was made to the Camanachd Association asking for the game to be replayed on the mainland, but they backed the referee, and Beauly — champions of Scotland for two years and fully convinced they were heading for their third victory — were out of the Cup on a technical decision. The Skye weather and the confusion in which the match ended had seen the local team into the next round of the competition, but there was to be a backlash from Beauly's smouldering resentment. They tried to call a general meeting of the Camanachd Association — which needed the assent of three-quarters of the 24 clubs in membership — to discuss their grievance, and they almost succeeded. Sixteen clubs supported them; obviously Beauly were not the only team who did not want to face the island elements.

Skye travelled to Strathpeffer on Wednesday 1 February 1899 to play Caberfeidh next day in the district final of the Cup. Attracted by the furore about Beauly's demise some 600 spectators turned up at Castle Leod to watch what turned out to be "a very mediocre game of shinty." The cup-winning team of the previous year, with only one change, were not able to repeat their performance, and only stalwart defensive work by Alex Murchison and Angus Macleod, and some courageous goal-keeping by Angus Ross saved them from a rout. Caberfeidh had the ball in the net within four minutes of the start and, after one brief foray by Skye, sustained the pressure.

> The Cabers had hard lines in not scoring, the half-backs were feeding the forwards in good style, and were it not for the miraculous saving of their goalkeeper, Portree would have been beaten time and again. He rushed out, and mingling with the players (a dangerous proceeding were the shooting of the Cabers more perfect), cleared time and again. From one of these encounters he was seen to limp back to his goal, having received a nasty knock on the knee. Only on rare occasions, even when encouraged by such cries as "Keep your place, Clachar", mingled with choice epithets from the language of Rob Donn, did the Islesmen break away, and when they did their shooting was blind.

Even so, Caberfeidh only had a 1-0 lead at half-time, and Norrie Robertson equalised for Skye shortly after the re-start. Thereafter, though, it was one-way traffic, even though one of the Cabers players was sent off for talking back to the referee, much to the displeasure of the home crowd. At the end Skye were down 4-1 and their erratic, weather-beaten Camanachd Cup run was over.

But at least they were now free to concentrate on defending their MacTavish trophy, they may well have consoled themselves as they boarded the homeward train next day. Their opponents in the first round were to be Lovat, who were reputed to be playing exceptionally well. Then, as they lined up at Strathcarron on Friday 10 March, the weather played up for the third time that season.

> The day was most unfavourable, rain pouring in torrents, and this was accompanied by a strong gale which blew obliquely across the field of play. The pitch was one of the most rugged ever seen, being liberally sprinkled all over with stones and mole-hills, and intersected in every conceivable direction with furrows.

In such conditions and on such a surface anything approaching skilful shinty was impossible. Lovat, much the heavier of the two teams, kept the Skye backs, Murchison and Macleod, "working like Trojans" for the first 20 minutes, but without scoring since "the strong wind rendered the deadliest shots for goal abortive". Eventually the Lovat forwards managed to scramble two goals and they led by that margin at half-time. After the break they renewed their pressure, scoring a third goal but losing their full forward when he twisted his knee in a tussle with a mole-hill! The Lovat backs, complaining of the cold, moved upfield looking for action and gave Farquhar Stewart a chance to break away and score for Skye, and that "seemed to enliven them, and for some time after they played a grand game; but the Lovat defence on the alert was impregnable." With that 3-1 defeat Skye's dreams of retaining the MacTavish Cup for a second year were at an end. Beauly, in fact, were to win it; a small consolation perhaps for having been blocked by Skye in the more prestigious Camanachd Cup.

For Skye the first phase of development was coming to an end as the old century gave way to the new. Some of the veterans who had formed the backbone of the team from its early Portree Athletic days were putting by their camans; others had left or were leaving the island. A report of a fund-raising dance in November 1899 says: "The club is this year making a rather desperate venture for the Camanachd trophy, as most of their veteran players are not expected to be in the team, and the honour of the club will be left solely in the hands of the young and rising talent of Portree." In fact, the "desperate venture" never took place; the team took part in no competitive games in the 1899-1900 season, and there is no record of any local activity either. In a sense, the club seemed to suffer a bout of exhaustion.

The previous season, with its atrocious weather and legacy of controversy over the Beauly match, had also been an extremely costly one, as indeed had the season before. Playing in two competitions on the mainland had raised the club's annual budget to well over £50, a sum which was difficult to raise despite the

1904 - 1905   **30**

By Jno. MacPherson as per a/c	1	15
By Norman "Tight" Cutting field		5
" Jno. MacPherson as per a/c	11	9
" do	5	7
" do	12	9
" Tickets to Garve for Team	3 . 6
" Breakfast at Kyle Hotel		16
" Canvas Shoes at Kyle		8 . 6
" Wm. McLennan (Lodgings for Bernisdale players)		10
" Garve Hotel Expenses	3 - 6
" Dinner in Boat		15
" Entrance Fee (Camanachd Ass'n. Postages		10
" Rule Books 1903 - 1904	1	6 . 3
"		3
" do 1904 - 1905		2
" Expenses at Garve half paid by fought		4
" Bernisdale players "Mail" fare		4
" Jno. MacPherson as per a/c	— 6 9
" Expenses of Team at Bernisdale thrash	18	8
" Jno. MacPherson as per a/c	1	13 . 9
" do	1	8 . 3
" Angus McLeod "Cutting field"		4
" Howden & Coy Wreath	1	1 . 6
" Jno. McGuire's a/c for Stationery		2
" Freight etc on Shinties		3
" Outlays by Secretary	1	10 .
" Balance at Credit	7	18 . 4
	29	7 . 4

Club expenses for the 1904-05 season. The Bernisdale men in the team got mail-coach fares to Portree and overnight lodgings to be ready for the morning steamer. The team hire to Bernisdale may indicate an unrecorded visit by the Portree team. The wreath was for the funeral of club chieftain Harry Macdonald, Viewfield.

generosity of patrons, the main source of income (The dance in aid of the "desperate venture" achieved a 16s loss!). Twenty years were to pass before the club again tried to budget on such an ambitious scale. And when Skye returned to competitive shinty in the 1900-01 season the decision had been taken that they could only afford to participate in one competition, despite the fact that this cut opportunities for sharpening their skills against top-class teams. So in the autumn of 1900 they bought some balls from John Grant, the local saddler, for 10s 9d; ordered camans worth £3 2s 6d from John Macpherson's Stores, Inverness; and set about practising for the forthcoming season's Camanachd competition — only to find themselves at the centre of more controversy and without a match until the spring of next year!

At first they seemed to be on the fringes of the row, their only fault being that they and Sutherland had been given byes in the northern district first round, while Inverness County had been drawn against Beauly (the winners to play Skye away), and Lovat against Caberfeidh (the winners to play Sutherland). Both Beauly and Inverness protested that the draw was in breach of rules since byes should only apply when an odd number of clubs was involved (and presumably in this case should have been held back till the second round). Failing redress both threatened to withdraw; Beauly in fact did so, while Inverness did not but scratched from the second round when Skye refused to give up home advantage to play on the mainland. Lovat, having been awarded the tie when Caberfeidh scratched in the first round, beat Sutherland in the second round - and then scratched rather than take the highway west to meet Skye in the district final! The effect of this highly contagious and farcical outbreak of scratching was that Skye — having been given a first round bye, and awarded the second and third round ties by default — were now in the semi-final of the Camanachd Cup without having swung a caman in the competition, or indeed in any other competition for the past two years! And they had been drawn against no less opponents than Kingussie, the current holders of the trophy!

Had Skye decided to cap the farce by themselves scratching they could hardly have been blamed. Instead, as the deadline of Saturday 15 March 1901 approached, the *Northern Chronicle's* local correspondent reported some intense practice sessions in Portree as captain John Mackinnon, Glenmore, tried to weld together "a practically new team". Only he, the two veterans Billy Ross and Kenneth Macrae, who had been persuaded to make one final appearance for Skye, and Norrie Robertson and Willoughby Dunn (taking over from Angus Ross in goal) had previous competition experience. The other seven were Archie Campbell, Sam Fraser, M Macdonald, D Macintyre, N Macintosh, D Macdougall and J Munro. As they stepped onto the pitch at the Longman in Inverness on a mild, bright afternoon just made for shinty, the hundreds who had travelled north from Badenoch by special trains thought the result a foregone conclusion, especially when they noted that "Kingussie were by far the stronger in physique and looked more athletic than their opponents, some of whom were by no means stalwart." As it happened they were proved right, and by a margin of 6-1, but not without a stubborn fight by Skye.

Kingussie were fast to attack and had a goal to their credit in the opening minutes. Despite some "sterling play" by the Skye backs — John Mackinnon and newcomer Archie Campbell — and Sam Fraser at half-back, another was to follow within a short time, largely because Dunn was insecure in goal and frequently left it unprotected. But at least this second reverse put some spirit into Skye:—

> Not long after they were awarded a foul. The ball was well sent in and Ross smartly scored, loud cheers being accorded the Island men on their success. To the close of the period the game was keenly contested. Kingussie showed the superior play, their fine long striking being of service. It was owing to the stubbornness of the Skyemen's defence, which improved as the game proceeded, that no further points were secured by the Badenoch men, who only led by one goal at half-time.

Skye started well in the second half, more than holding their own for a long period and, indeed, almost equalising. For a while they tested the Kingussie defence, and at that stage those who had written Skye off before the game began "would not have cared to wager how the match would finish." But gradually Kingussie's superior strength and experience began to tell, and they got a third and a fourth goal, with two more to follow in the closing stages of the game. But for a young and inexperienced team Skye's performance had been by no means bad, and their determination won the respect of mainland critics who reckoned that "had they had more practice the score against them might have been much less." That was the type of verdict Skye were to hear only too often over the next few years.

In fact, Skye's opportunities for practice against top class mainland opposition were once more to diminish rather than increase, and for the old, familiar reason — their isolated location was again to be an excuse for penalising them. The blow fell at the Camanachd Association's annual meeting in September 1901. The Beauly delegate, no doubt still smarting at the memory of the gale-swept farce in Portree three years earlier, moved that all ties with Skye should be played on the mainland at a place to be named by the Association's council; there was immediate support from the Lovat delegate. In the absence of a Skye representative delegates from Perth and Glasgow tried to argue the manifest unfairness of such a proposal but to no avail; they were defeated 15-4 on a vote. Obviously a number of teams were quite prepared to face the possibility of forcing Skye out of first-class shinty, rather than face the cost and inconvenience of travelling to the island. More than 20 years and a World War were to pass before Skye again played in front of their home supporters.

The club's response to this setback was to enter immediately for the Camanachd Cup. As the fates would have it, both they and Beauly were given byes in the first round — and then drawn against each other in the second round! The match was originally scheduled for a Saturday but when Skye protested that this would mean them remaining on the mainland until Monday they were given a concession. In future all Skye games would be played on a weekday, and if this made it more difficult to raise a team at least that same difficulty would apply to both clubs involved.

The Beauly game took place at Strathcarron on Friday 17 January 1902 and the only report of it is brief — perhaps mercifully so since Skye lost 6-0! Suffice it to say that Skye, with only three of the previous year's semi-finalists available, "were outplayed at almost every point, and at goal they were very weak." With a new generation of young, inexperienced players, the club was again faced with the problem that had beset it when it first entered competitive shinty seven years earlier — how to gain the skills to beat their mainland peers when they only met them once a year? There was also a feeling that the club was still much too dependent on the village of Portree, though here the revival of the Bernisdale club in 1901 might help. Certainly that was the mood that emerged from the annual meeting held in November 1902: "The feasibility of introducing new players from outlying districts was discussed, it being pointed out that the designation of the club brought the whole of the island within its sphere. Ultimately it was agreed to extend every encouragement to the club formed at Bernisdale last season with a view to selecting some players therefrom for the forthcoming contests."

These contests turned out to be only four in number in the four years from 1903 onwards. Whatever fickle fate ruled the Camanachd Cup draw had obviously got the message that Skye and Beauly had seen enough of each other recently, and now dictated that in each of the next four years Skye meet Lovat! As it turned out this was doing the islanders no great favour. Lovat at the time had a strong and experienced team and each year brought Skye's further cup ambitions to an abrupt halt. Not that the matches were bad. The first three were excellent games, although they seemed to conform to a pattern. Apart from the fact that they were held on a farm field at Garve, Skye started off brightly and bravely in all of them but the heavier team's stamina told in the end.

The first of the Lovat clashes took place on a drizzly Friday afternoon in January 1903. Skye quickly found the net and for much of the first half gave their opponents the run-around, but without further scoring. As the second half progressed Lovat stamina began to pay dividends on the heavy turf and they ran out eventual 4-1 winners, though "the score hardly indicated the run of play." The following year's encounter, at the same venue on Friday 8 January 1904, was every bit as evenly matched, according to the *Inverness Courier*:—

> Lovat led by a goal at half-time. By superb play the Skyemen equalised early in the second period, and showed if anything smarter play than their opponents. The Lovat team were, however, the stronger, and ultimately got the lead. Up till the close of the game the Skyemen fought pluckily, but they could not overthrow the Lovat players who were ultimately the winners, the scores being - Lovat,2; Skye,1.

The *Chronicle's* correspondent was even more flattering to the islanders, claiming that "certain it is that their display on Friday was their best in their history as a club." This he ascribed to the presence in the team of four ex-Caberfeidh players, the brothers Peter D and John C Robertson, D Mackenzie and D Forbes. Peter Robertson (usually known as PD) had four years earlier taken over the lease of the Scorrybreck estate, and was to have a lasting influence over Skye shinty.

With two such performances behind them, and the acclaim of the usually critical Inverness press, Skye, with "a lot of young, lithe players", must have had high hopes of finally laying the Lovat jinx when they left the Kyle train at Garve on Friday 13 January 1905. From the moment the referee blew the whistle "the play was very keen and fast, and there was little to choose between the teams." Lovat scored the first goal, soon to be countered by Skye who went on to score a second shortly afterwards, only to have Lovat equalise a minute later. At half-time the score stood 2-2, though Skye were acknowledged to have had the better of the play. The pace remained fast for most of the second half, but gradually Lovat stamina again began to show, and paid off in a final score-line of 4-2. The *Courier* was full of praise for the Skye attack:—

> The forwards, especially Cumming, were showing 'cute' play. Norman Robertson and Peter Robertson excelled, but they could not overcome the strong defence.... The match was well contested and Lovat, although having slightly the better staying power, were not two goals better than their opponents in point of play. The match was contested in sportsmanlike style, and there was hardly a trace of rough play.

Skye must inevitably have been disappointed — hopes of a third-time lucky strike had proved to be Black Friday the 13th after all, and no amount of press plaudits could make up for the lack of a result. But at least they had re-entered the MacTavish competition, and with such a lively and skilled team (and Lovat well out of the way!) they could reasonably expect to beat Contin next month and, who knows, repeat the glory days of '98! Alas, it was not to be: the *Northern Chronicle* broke the dismal news that the club "was compelled to scratch, as it was found at the last moment impossible to get up a team.....Shinty enthusiasm, however, still runs high, and on Saturday a match was played between the Veterans and Juniors, resulting in a victory by the former by 2-1. Next year it is hoped Skye will be represented by a fine lot of smart players in the national competition."

In the three matches with Lovat over the three years Skye had used a pool of 23 players who had given a good account of themselves. Clearly there was a wealth of young shinty talent in the island at the time. The difficulty — as the use of so many players in so short a time shows, and the withdrawal from the MacTavish Cup underlines — was to have them available for two-day mid-week trips to mainland venues. Never was the unfairness of the ban on home games so starkly illustrated. Nor were the hopes of "a fine lot of smart players" finding themselves among next year's trophy contenders to be fulfilled. Half a dozen new names had to be added to the existing pool to enable the club to field a team against (yes, inevitably!) Lovat in the Camanachd Cup encounter at Strathcarron on Friday 2 February 1906. Among the familiar mole-hills, now churned into a quagmire by a blinding snowstorm, the light, young and relatively inexperienced Skye boys found themselves at the wrong end of an 8-1 onslaught. But not without a bit of style:—

> The opening was sensational, Skye taking up the running from the throw up, rushing down on Mann and scoring ere the game was thirty seconds old. For quite ten minutes Skye forced the pace and gave the Lovat men a hot time of it, the play being pretty evenly divided. The result, however, was only to wear themselves down, for no team could long withstand such a pace on such heavy ground.....

And of course Skye didn't. Slowly and surely Lovat's effective tackling and hitting asserted themselves and at half-time Skye were 4-1 down, and by full time Lovat had added another four. But at least the *Northern Chronicle's* correspondent could understand the islanders' problems better than the Camanachd Association:—

> It must not be forgotten that the Skyemen have much to contend with. They are isolated, and have no chance of practice with other teams, while their opponents have already carried off two cups this season. The Skyemen are nothing if not plucky, and always toe the line, and nobody would grudge them the success which their dogged determination deserves, but which fate has so far denied them.

But the club had now used around 30 players in four matches; obviously it could not continue to blood young talent at such a rate on the basis of a once-a-year visit to the mainland. Skye's participation in competitive shinty had reached a critical stage. In season 1906-07 no Skye team appeared in any of the national competitions.

Skye teams, 1899-1906

02/02/99 (v Caberfeidh, Camanachd Cup)
Angus Ross, Murchison and Macleod, Ferguson, A Mackenzie, J Mackenzie and William Ross, K Macrae, W Dunn, N Robertson and F Stewart

10/03/99 (v Lovat, MacTavish Cup)
Goal, William Maclean; backs, Angus Macleod, Alex Murchison (captain); half-backs, Neil Macintosh, Norman Macleod, John Munro, and William Munro; forwards, Farquhar Stewart, Angus Ross, Norrie Robertson, Murdo Ferguson and John Mackinnon .

15/03/01 (v Kingussie, Camanachd Cup)
Goal, W M Dunn; N Robertson, William Ross, Ken Macrae, John Mackinnon, A Campbell, S Fraser, M Macdonald, D Macintyre, N Macintosh, D Macdougall, and J Munro.

17/01/02 (v Beauly, Camanachd Cup)
Goal, D A Mackenzie; backs, Norman Robertson and A Campbell (captain); half-backs, William Maclean, A Nicolson, D Macdougall and P Stewart; forwards, J Maclean, A Mackenzie, J Nicolson, A Campbell and R Kemp.

23/01/03 (v Lovat, Camanachd Cup)
Arch Campbell(capt); John Mackinnon; D Macdougall; P Murchison; S Matheson; A Campbell; J Maclean; N Robertson; A Maclean; M Maclean; D Macintyre and R Kemp

08/01/04 (v Lovat, Camanachd Cup)
D Macdougall, D Forbes, A M Murchison, John C Robertson, Peter Robertson, Neil Robertson, P Murchison, J Maclean, A Maclean, D Mackenzie, A Campbell and D Macintyre

13/01/05 (v Lovat, Camanachd Cup)
C Macleod, J Robertson, D Forbes, Peter Robertson, Matheson, D Maclean, James Macrae, Norman Robertson, R Macdonald, Neil Macleod, Macintyre and J Cumming.

02/02/06 (v Lovat, Camanachd Cup)
D Macintyre, R Macdonald, J Cumming, E Macleod, W Kemp, A M Murchison, F Kemp, M Grant, A Mackenzie, D Forbes, J Robertson and J Cameron

Chapter 5

The Robertson Cup

The club needed all the pluck and determination at its command to meet the crisis, which seems to have been much more than a matter of getting together a team that could spare the time to play on the mainland. During the 1905-06 season their funds had sunk to £11 9s 4d, the lowest since their foundation, and most of that was a credit balance from the previous year. Members' and patrons' subscriptions, the sole source of regular income, were not collected, suggesting a complete breakdown in administration. But the accounts from November 1906 onwards show a renewed drive for membership and suggest the club was once again moving with purpose.

Meanwhile the problem remained of providing players with more exposure to competitive shinty than an annual foray to the mainland. Fortunately, the man to match the occasion was on hand — Peter D Robertson of Scorrybreck, whose spirited performances for recent Skye teams had been noted by the press. At a committee meeting on Wednesday 26 December 1906 the Skye Camanachd Club welcomed an offer from him to present a cup for competition among island teams, his main stipulation being that at least three teams must enter. "This is an offer which should induce young men throughout the island to organise themselves, as the opportunities for competition will now become more frequent than could be the case if teams had to go out of the island for opponents," wrote the *Northern Chronicle's* local correspondent. "Portree has been upholding the ancient game against the mainland for a number of years, but local rivalry is much required...." Down the years the Robertson Cup competition was to prove the truth of that statement. At times when Skye's fortunes in major competitions were at a low ebb it was to keep the pulse of shinty beating in the island.

The response to the new stimulus was immediate as the club set about salvaging the remainder of the season by organising the first competition. Three dozen shinty sticks were ordered from John Macpherson, Inverness, for the district teams, and Mr Macpherson — a Badenoch man with a lifelong enthusiasm for shinty apart from his professional interest as a sports-shop owner — presented a silver-mounted caman for the captain of the winning team. Five teams entered — Portree, Portree Juniors, Braes, Bernisdale and Edinbane, and Portree Juniors were drawn away against Edinbane in the first round, the other three teams being awarded byes. And so on Saturday 23 February 1907, amidst "a great deal of local interest" the two teams met on a field provided by R L Robertson Macleod of Greshornish — perhaps the same "green grounds of Coishletter" on which his ancestor promoted the New Year game 41 years earlier — for the first encounter of the Robertson Cup.

The local team had the advantage in physique, and their bustling rushes never allowed the visitors — who showed superior smartness in hitting — to settle down to their usual game. Continuing on the aggressive, the Edinbane men had the bulk of play in the visitors' territory during the greater portion of the first half, and at length Gillies scored a clever goal. At this stage Portree had the misfortune to part with the services of Macleod, their back, who retired slightly hurt, and half-time saw the local team leading by a goal. Playing with eleven men in the second division of the game, the visitors seemed in no wise daunted, although Gillies quickly notched a second goal for his side. At this stage the Portree forwards took the game in hand, and, for the first time, showed any real signs of combined play. Fraser, Boyd, and M Stewart scored in rapid succession, and a fourth goal by the first-named player, shortly before time, enabled the Portree Juniors to enter the second round for the cup.

Unfortunately, local correspondents were not to prove as diligent as the *Chronicle's* man in Edinbane in recording the fortunes of the Robertson Cup. Reporting was extremely erratic, some brief accounts even omitting scores, and in some years the competition went unreported though it probably took place. When Portree and Braes met at Portree in the second round of the competition a

Peter Donald Robertson (1880-1956) here seen (third from left) squiring the Duke of Sutherland, the Prince of Wales and the Duke of York at an agricultural show shortly after World War 1. PD, as he was familiarly known, mixed as easily with crofters and farmers as he did with royalty. He belonged to a Perthshire family which had extensive farming interests in Ross-shire and Sutherland, leasing a number of sheep farms and working them from a main base at Achilty. He was also a keen sportsman, and a golfer of professional standard. PD leased the large Scorrybreck estate - cleared in 1840 and latterly leased to the Stewarts of Ensay - from Lord Macdonald around the turn of the century. During his tenure he enjoyed a reputation as a generous and considerate employer, and after World War 1 he gave up the lease to allow the estate to be returned to crofting tenure. In so doing he also incidentally benefitted Skye shinty for a number of prominent players of the post-World War 2 era were to come from the townships of Torvaig and Achachorc.

week after the Edinbane game the reporter was as interested in the weather — "delightful" — and the large number of spectators as he was in the match, which he summed up in a single sentence: "The local team had matters all their own way throughout; they did not, in fact, appear to take the game seriously, and ran out easy winners by 8 goals to 0." A fortnight later Bernisdale and Portree Juniors met on the same pitch, though this time it was "a perfect quagmire" because of recent heavy rains. "The visitors were a sturdy set, and from the start of the game they assumed the aggressive," the *Chronicle* notes. "Within ten minutes of the start they had the ball in the net, and an easy win followed." Presumably by a greater margin than 1-0, though that is not recorded.

Fine weather brought "several hundreds" of spectators to Portree on the last Saturday in March to watch the final between Bernisdale and the home team, no doubt expecting a hard contest after the display Bernisdale had put up against Portree Juniors in the previous round. Nor were they disappointed.

> From the outset play of a fast nature was witnessed, and it was early evident that the visitors meant to force the pace, and also that the teams suffered from an over-anxiety to score, and consequently there was some erratic shooting by both sides. Portree proved supreme alike in tactics, agility, and combination, when occasion arose, and the game ended in their favour by 4 goals to 0. The one-sided nature of the scoring is, however, by no means a true index to the run of the play. The visitors were worthy of, at any rate, a couple of goals in the second half, but the home defence could not be penetrated.

At that evening's festivities in the Portree Hotel, when Major A D Mackinnon, chieftain of Skye Camanachd, presented the Robertson Cup to Sandy Mackenzie, the Portree captain, few could doubt that the new competition had been a complete success in its first season. The touchline crowds reported at the matches were sufficient evidence that local loyalties had been roused and engaged, and the rivalry that burned so intensely between the Portree and Bernisdale teams down to the 1950s probably stems from that cup final, the first recorded clash between the clubs apart from a youth match in 1898. Major Mackinnon was on firm ground in hoping that teams would be formed in other centres throughout the island and that "a strong combination might thus be available for the Scottish Cup (i.e., the Camanachd Cup) next season."

One new team, Dunvegan, appeared in the competition in the 1907-08 season, and although there are no reports of Braes or Bernisdale certainly one and probably both took part and were ousted by Portree or Portree Juniors in the early stages. In the first round Dunvegan were at home to Edinbane on a November Saturday so wet that the downpour delayed the start until 3.30pm, when it was agreed to play a half-hour each way. The more experienced Edinbane team pressed from the start and led 3-0 at half-time and, despite some attacking forays by Dunvegan at the start of the second half, were to emerge 7-0 winners at the final whistle

In the second round in mid-December Edinbane were defeated 3-2 at home to Portree but lodged an official protest because the game had run five minutes over time, and Portree's winning goal had come in that period. As it turned out, they might have saved face by accepting the result. In the replay, before "several hundred spectators" on a frost-bound Portree pitch on Saturday 4 January 1908, they toppled to a 9-0 defeat. In the final, on 15 February, Portree met Portree Juniors and, in a game which "did not appear to raise any great enthusiasm on the part of the meagre crowd who lined the ropes," beat them by a 6-2 margin, thus winning the Robertson Cup for the second time. Presumably the meagre attendance, compared with the hundreds who had watched Bernisdale the previous year, reflects the lack of rivalry in a game between what were virtually Portree's first and second teams. (Indeed, the local correspondent refers to them incongruously as the "1st XI" and the "2nd XI", which may help to explain the inadequacy of the few shinty reports from Skye at the time!)

The information that can be found for the 1908-09 season is even sketchier. *The Northern Chronicle* of Wednesday 10 February 1909 carries the following brief note:-

> Camanachd - Skye Cup. - In view of their tie with the Braes team next Saturday, the Portree "A" team are daily practising. The Portree "B" team, which were drawn against Edinbane in the same round, were disqualified, owing to their failure to turn up at Skeabost last week to play their match, so that Edinbane now enter the final.

The 1907 Portree 1st team, first winners of the Robertson Cup. Back row, l-r:- Lawrence Skene; Sergeant Scott; Donald "Ben" Macdougall; ? ; A Murchison; Kenneth Macrae; Billy Ross. Middle row:- A D Mackinnon; Rory Kemp; Ewen "Rocais" Macdougall; ? ; ? ; J G Mackay. Front row:- Finlay Kemp; D "Curdy" Macdougall; Sandy Mackenzie (captain); Willie Kemp; Murdo Maclean. The three unidentified players are Alex Macmillan, L Macvicar and Campbell, though in what order is not known.

Since these were obviously second round ties it may well be that another team or teams — perhaps Bernisdale or Dunvegan — were beaten in the first round. The *Chronicle's* report of the Braes game, which took place on 20 February 1909, is equally brief:-

> The semi-final in this competition was played on the Public Park here on Saturday afternoon before a large number of spectators, the competing teams being Portree "A" team and Braes, when the former won by three hails to one. The losers put up a splendid fight.

And there, unfortunately and tantalisingly, the press information dries up. No report has been found of the final, so we may never know if Portree won the trophy for the third time, or if Edinbane were successful.

For the 1909-10 season, on the other hand, we know the finalists in the competition, but know nothing of the preliminary rounds. Attracted by good weather, a large crowd turned out to watch Braes and the Colonials fight for the cup in Portree on Saturday 5 March 1910. Presumably to awaken some spirit of local loyalty, Portree had abandoned the "A" and "B" formula and divided its shinty resources on a territorial basis. Thus were born two teams with the unlikely names of the Academicals and the Colonials, the former representing the centre of the village, while the latter drew their players and support from the rural hinterland around Lotts and Fisherfield and Sluggans — wild colonials in the eyes of the townies! But wild or otherwise, the Colonials found themselves under intense pressure from the Braes men for the first quarter-hour of the game, and eventually conceded a goal, though they managed to equalise shortly afterwards.

> Play now became more general, both teams striving to get the lead. Fraser, for Braes, did splendid work, all his shots landing in the goal-mouth, and he kept his forwards supplied with plenty chances of scoring. Macinnes played a hard game, and was the means of a second goal being scored by Mackintosh for Braes. The Colonials now did some pressing, and their dashing forward, Lorn, scored after a brilliant run through the half-backs and backs of the Braes team. At half-time the teams crossed over with two hails each. The second half was stubbornly contested, and both goals were assailed in turn. Macpherson and Macqueen, the Braes backs, put in good work, and Macdougall and Mackenzie for the Colonials. Fraser again shone, and a beautiful shot of his, delivered from the half-back division, was, after a scrimmage in the mouth of the goal, put through by Matheson, and the match resulted in a victory for Braes by 3 hails to 2.

The sports pages for the 1910-11 season yield two match reports, both of them for first round ties. On Saturday 12 November 1910 the Academicals travelled to Edinbane, no doubt with high hopes of giving their country cousins a lesson in the art of the caman. But it was not to be, even though the Academicals scored the only goal in an evenly contested first half.

> On resuming Edinbane speedily proved the aggressors, and scored their first goal in the first few minutes of the game, and thereafter continued to have the game in their own hands, although very ably defended by the Academicals , which was a much lighter team. Peter Graham, in his usual good form, did excellent work, and his long shots proved the undoing of the opposing team. When the whistle sounded the score stood 5 to 1 in favour of Edinbane. Very plucky play was made by Gillanders and Mackenzie, backs, and Ross, Boyd, and Baxter, half-backs, against Edinbane, while some excellent play was made for Edinbane by Peter Graham, Duncan Graham, Norman Macleod and Lachlan Gillies.

A week later Braes met the Colonials in Portree on a fine Saturday which pulled out the crowds, but with a hard frost which made the players' footing anything but secure. The first half was evenly fought and ended with no score.

> On resuming the Colonials pressed and scored their first goal through Macvicar, who nicely turned the ball into the Braes goalkeeper from a pass from Lorn. After this the game became rather faster. Murdo Maclean in the half forward division did splendid work for the Colonials. John Maclean was enabled to score a second goal for the Colonials towards the end of the game, and the whistle blew for time with the score - Colonials, 2; Braes, 0. The Braes backs played very well, but the forward line was very weak. The Colonials now meet the Edinbane team in the second round for the cup.

Obviously another second round tie was scheduled involving two other teams — probably, on past record, Bernisdale and Dunvegan, though it is just possible that a Glenmore team had made its appearance unheralded by the press, the glen at that time being a populous area with fairly prosperous crofting townships. Certainly, in the 1911-12 competition, a Glenmore team is recorded losing 6-3 to Braes in the first round in December 1911, while Edinbane beat Portree 3-2 in another first round tie in the same month. Unfortunately, nothing further appears about the progress of the competition to the cup finals of 1911 and

The Robertson Cup-winning Braes team of 1910. Back row, l-r: Finlay Kemp, Skye Camanachd; Alec Macintosh (Sandy Chaluim); William Macqueen (Uilleam Dhiarmaid); James Beaton, Portree; William Ross, Portree; William Nicolson (Uilleam Ruadh); Malcolm Michie, Camustianavaig; John Macinnes (Seonachan Bean 'ic Uilleim); Norman Beaton, Portree. Front row, l-r: Angus Ross, Skye Camanachd; Duncan Macpherson (Duchan Lachlainn Uilleim); Lachlan Macinnes (Lachie Dhomhnaill Lachlainn: D M "Doosie" Fraser; William Macpherson (Uilleam Lachlainn Uilleim); Kenny Macrae, Skye Camanachd.

1912; all that can be said with a fair deal of certainty is that shinty in Skye during these years seems to have been in a much healthier state than sports reporting! But one other interesting little snippet is worth a mention; on Saturday 18 March 1911 Bernisdale travelled to Uig for a friendly match with the local team, the first match there since the Uig team had begun to practice the previous winter "in accordance with Association rules." So clearly an Uig team had a mind to enter for the Robertson Cup in the 1911-12 season; whether they actually did so is unfortunately not on record.

All that is recorded of the 1912-13 competition is a cursory report of Bernisdale and Braes meeting in the final on Saturday 8 March 1913, presumably at Portree though that is not stated.

> Unfortunately the weather was very unsuitable, but both teams showed characteristic pluck and dash in spite of the elements. After an exceedingly hard game Bernisdale emerged winners by 3 hails to 1. In the evening the cup was presented to Mr Murchison, captain of the Bernisdale Club, by Mr W J Robertson, president of the Skye Camanachd Club.

During the 1913-14 season no mention of the Robertson Cup seems to have appeared in the routine district coverage of Skye affairs in the Inverness-based weekly press. But given the obvious gaps in reporting local shinty matches in the preceding years, apart from 1907 when the competition was fresh and exciting, that is no reason to suppose that it did not take place. Even with the erratic records available it is obvious that the competition had a major and positive impact on shinty in Skye in the seven years leading up to World War 1. Places where shinty had been a traditional festive sport — such as Bernisdale, Braes and Edinbane — had joined Portree in bringing a modern competitive edge to the game. The revival had touched Dunvegan and Uig, and even a relatively small community like Glenmore had been emboldened to try its luck.

Admittedly, the Robertson influence had not yet spread to the southern end of Skye, though that was to happen after the war. Communications were probably the main stumbling block. While a Portree team could travel comfortably to Edinbane in the Portree Hotel char-a-banc (at a cost of £1 8s 4d in 1910), play a game of shinty, enjoy some post-match hospitality and still return home at a reasonable hour, Breakish or Tarscavaig would have have been just out of reach. The steep gradients of the old Druim nan Cleoc road were crueller to early internal combustion engines than they were to horses, and taking the steamer to Broadford and travelling onward by road was a cumbersome business. Clearly the needs of local shinty teams were not high on the priority list when Skye's geography was created!

But apart from generating local enthusiasm for the game, the Robertson Cup had also created a pool of players with some experience of competitive shinty. An entry of five or six teams a year meant that between 60 and 72 players at the very least were directly involved, and local practice matches probably involved many more. Even at a time when natural skills and traditional methods were more valued than formal training, local rivalry was keen enough to ensure that some practice was undertaken. In Portree, the Volunteers' drill instructor, Sergeant Kennedy — who also played for the "B" team — put the players through the paces of routine military gymnastic training. And as the pool of talent available to the Skye Camanachd Club grew wider, the nearer it came to its aim of representing the whole island and the less dependent it became on a nucleus of players around Portree. By the time World War 1 brought competitive shinty to a halt, enthusiasts of the game in Skye already had good reason to bless the name of Peter D Robertson.

ROBERTSON CUP TEAMS

1906-1907

EDINBANE - 23/02/07: Donald Maclean, Rod. Ross, Norman Ross, Donald Macneill, Lach. Gillies, Ewen Gillies, Donald Gillies (captain), Peter Macdonald, Donald Silver, Sam. Maclean, Donald Maclean and John Macrae.

PORTREE JUNIORS - 23/02/07: Donald Bain, Ewen Macleod, James Cumming, Norman Beaton, John Macinnes (captain), John Stewart, Norman Mackinnon, Murdo Mackenzie, Murdo Stewart, Donald Fraser, Alex Campbell and James Boyd.

BERNISDALE - 16/03/07: Goal, D A Munro; backs, Norman Macleod and M Sutherland; half-backs, Peter Graham, Archibald Maclean and Dugald Matheson; centres, Sam Matheson, D Beaton and D Macleod; forwards, A Macleod, Wm Armstrong, and D W Macleod.

PORTREE - 30/03/07: Goal, E Macdougall; backs, D A Boyd and Finlay Kemp; half-backs, John Orme , Alexander Mackenzie (captain) and Alex Macmillan; centres, Rod Macdonald, Rod Kemp and Murdo Maclean; forwards, Lach. Macvicar, Arch. Campbell and William Kemp.

BERNISDALE - 30/03/07: Goal, J Maclean; backs, Norman Macleod and M Sutherland; half-backs, Peter Graham, Arch Maclean (captain) and D Matheson; centres, M Graham, D A Munro and Sam Matheson; forwards, Alex Macleod, D M Macleod and David Macleod.

1907-1908

EDINBANE - 16/11/07: Donald Maclean (captain), Hugh Gillies, Peter Graham, Charles Stewart, Neil Mackinnon, John Maclean, Donald Silver, Lachlan Gillies, John Macinnes, Donald Macneil, Donald Macfarlane, Charles Macewan.

DUNVEGAN - 16/11/07: John Mackinnon, Angus Macphee, Donald Macphee, Donald Mackinnon, H Maclean, D Macphee, A Macaskill, N Macphee, N Maclennan, J Macleod, Dugald Macleod, E Meikle.

PORTREE 1st XI - 15/02/08: Goal, Ewen Macdougall; backs, Finlay Kemp and Donald Macdougall; half-backs, M Maclean, Alex Macmillan and Alex Mackenzie; centres, Rod Kemp, A Murchison and D Macdougall; forwards, W Kemp (captain), Campbell and L Macvicar.

PORTREE 2nd XI - 15/02/08: Goal, Donald Bain; backs, Harry Mackinnon and Graham; half-backs, Lachlan Macinnes, John Macinnes and D Macintyre; centres, Ewen Macintosh, Norman Mackinnon and Sergt Kennedy; forwards, M Mackintosh, D Fraser (captain) and Norman Beaton.

1909-1910

BRAES - 05/03/10: D Macdougall, W Macpherson, W Macqueen, D M Fraser, J Beaton, W Nicolson, L Macinnes (captain), J Macinnes, J Macdonald, D Matheson, A Mackintosh, W Michie.

COLONIALS - 05/03/10: E Macdougall, D Macdougall (captain), A Mackenzie, J Macvicar, K Maclean, J Nicolson, M Maclean, J Maclean, John Lorn, M Macleod, L Macvicar, M Nicolson.

1910-1911

ACADEMICALS - 12/11/10: John Grant, Kenneth Gillanders (captain), William Macintyre, Peter Maclean, Jim Mackenzie, A W Ross, John Nicolson, Peter Boyd, Angus Baxter, Willie Fraser, Logan Orme, John Maclean.

EDINBANE - 12/11/10: Donald Maclean, Alex Macinnes, Norman Macfarlane, Peter Murchison, Peter Graham, Donald Gillies, Duncan Graham (captain), Sam Matheson, Hugh Gillies, Norman Macleod, Lachlan Gillies, John Maclean.

BRAES - 19/11/10: Alex Michie, Wm Macpherson, Wm Macqueen, H Nicolson, Wm Nicolson, J Nicolson, J Macdonald, J Macdonald, J MacCowan, D Macpherson, Wm Matheson and Nicolson.

COLONIALS - 19/11/10: Ewen Macdougall, D Macdougall, A Maclean, John Macvicar, M Macleod, M Maclean, A Macdougall, J Macdonald, L Macvicar, J Maclean, J Macdougall and Mackenzie.

Chapter 6

The Glasgow Skye

On the evening of Saturday 17 October 1903 a number of Skyemen, probably more than 20 of them, gathered in the Shepherd's Hall, Bath Street, Glasgow. Their purpose, noted in a new minute-book meticulously maintained until 1948, was to form a Glasgow Skye Camanachd Club and they set about it earnestly and efficiently. Within the next ten days they held three more meetings and by the end of the year had met seven times in all. By that time they had elected a committee, chosen a string of patrons that far outnumbered the home club's, rented a pitch, embarked on fund-raising ventures, and arranged their first match — a friendly with the well-established Glasgow Caledonian Shinty Club — for late January. At their first annual general meeting in June 1904 they felt confident enough to enter three competitions the following season — the Camanachd Cup, the Celtic Society Cup, and the Southern League.

But this wasn't the first flourish of Skye camans in Glasgow by any means. From the early decades of the nineteenth century a trickle of islanders had moved into the growing industrial city, and by the 1850s the trickle was swelling into a considerable flood. By 1865 there were enough of them to merit founding the Glasgow Skye Association to look after their social needs, and to help the continuing stream of young Skye people seeking employment in the city. Some of them would have taken their shinty skills with them, or if not — given the fluctuating health of the game in Skye at the time — have learned them from their elders already in the city. Almost certainly some Skye boys would have been involved in the shinty match for which Mairi Mhor nan Oran so lovingly baked the *bonnaich* at New Year 1876. Just over three years later, on Friday 21 March 1879, the *Highlander* newspaper carried an intriguing report about the demise of the Ossian Shinty Club:-

> We regret to learn that this Club has been broken up, but, Phoenix-like, from its ashes a new club has arisen which is to be called "The Skye Shinty Club." The Ossian Club had a short and chequered career and one cannot think of its origin and palmiest days without a pang of regret, for some of those who took an active part in its organisation are now no more. We refer particularly to the late John MacQueen who was its first secretary.

The following week the paper carried further news of the club's progress. John Nicolson had been elected chairman, Alex Gillies its treasurer, and JG Mackay — then working for a city merchant but already deeply involved in land politics — its secretary. A Finlay MacQueen from Braes — possibly related to John MacQueen of the old Ossian club — whose son and nephew, both Donald, played for the later Glasgow Skye club, was also involved. These stalwarts decided that "the uniform of the club is to be the kilt" and that all business meetings should be conducted in Gaelic!

In the ensuing months a little more information leaked northwards to the Inverness-based *Highlander*. By May it reported that "M'Leod of M'Leod has accepted the office of Chief of this young but energetic Club." By November it knew that Skye had beaten Glasgow Inverness in a friendly at Govan on the first of the month, but didn't carry the score. And on 21 November 1879 it carried a brief report of a match between Skye and Fingal:-

> These two kilted clubs met at Govan last Saturday afternoon. At the close of play the result stood Skye, 4; Fingal, none. Two of the hails were disputed and the game ended in darkness.

Next week the paper carried a rather abrupt letter to the effect that 55 minutes of the game had been played, the score had been 2-0, and no hails had been disputed! And there the northern papers seem to lose trace of the subsequent history of the club, though further intriguing snippets may well lie in dusty archives in Glasgow. How regularly it played is difficult to say, since shinty was only emerging as an organised competitive sport in the city. Certainly JG Mackay had moved back to Skye by 1886 and his forceful personality would have been missed. The club was last heard of in 1894 when the treasurer handed back to the Glasgow Skye Association the last of its funds, a sum of £1 11s 1d, presumably because it was now moribund and may have been so for some time.

The moving spirits in the 1903 revival were a new generation of Skyemen who had arrived in the city. Donald MacCowan from Braes, who had played for Skye in 1896, was the Glasgow Skye's first president, and John F Mackintosh its first captain. Others included Murdo Ferguson, also an ex-Skye player; Archie Macpherson, who was to play an active part as a club official for many years; and Charles Maclean, son of Tormod Beag of Land League fame who had now moved his joinery business from Portree to the city. They were all young men, some of them little more than 20, and eager for new ventures.

One of their earliest tasks was to choose colours for the team. Charles Maclean, no doubt imbued by his father's loyalty to the home team, was in favour of white shirts and blue shorts (or "knick-

GLASGOW SKYE CAMANACHD CLUB.

Office - Bearers.

Chief.
REGINALD MACLEOD, ESQ., OF MACLEOD, C.B.

President.
HUGH MACLEOD, ESQ.

Vice-Presidents.
MR. DONALD MACCOWAN.
MR. SAMUEL CAMPBELL.

Secretary.
MR. ALEXANDER MACPHERSON,
16 DALHOUSIE STREET.

Treasurer.
MR. DONALD MACINTOSH,
352 ST. VINCENT STREET.

An early membership card.

ers" as they were then known, and certainly they weren't short!). But the majority favoured maroon and white hooped jerseys, though the minutes do not explain the particular significance of that choice. Charles Maclean also wanted club membership confined to native Skyemen, but the committee, perhaps recalling the major contribution made by incomers to founding the home club, decided that "all interested in the game of shinty" should be eligible. That was a wise decision. Otherwise some of the club's most loyal and effective players and administrators would have been lost to it, notably John Macdonald from the Torridon area of Ross-shire who was one of the outstanding figures in its history. In its later days it was to depend heavily on players from all the shinty strongholds of the Highlands and particularly from the coastal strip from Lochcarron up to Shieldaig.

Then there were the problems of finding a playing field, raising funds and organising training sessions. In fact these proved to be perennial problems; the club was forever teetering on the brink of financial crisis, and every few years it was in search of a new home. It's first base was a park at Ruchill belonging to Flanagan Bros, farmers, on which it was allowed to play for an annual rental of £7. It recouped some of the outlay by allowing Glasgow University Shinty Club access to the field for a rental of £2 10s, "payable in advance"! By 1909 it had moved to Carmyle where it rented the ground of the Kenmuir Cricket Club for a sum of £10, but a year later it moved again, this time to a ground at Possilpark. Apart from these, it had a number of even more temporary pitches before it was forced to move on becuase the ground was needed for some other purpose — frequently urban development — or because the rental had soared beyond the club's financial reach.

The Glasgow Skye's financial reach seldom matched its ambitions. Apart from the annual rent burden its league and cup commitments meant fairly frequent visits to Edinburgh, Paisley and a number of rural outposts around the Cowal area, and in most seasons it also ran a reserve team. While its extensive list of patrons helped to set the club up at the outset, their long-term generosity seems to have fallen off, perhaps because many of them were also patrons of the home club and may well have given it preference when opening the purse strings. Although fund-raising events, such as ceilidhs, dances and smoking concerts were held, they tended to get lost in the busy social calendar of Glasgow Highlanders, and sometimes ran at a loss. Thus the Glasgow Skye's treasurer was forever cajoling recalcitrant members for their subscriptions. The 1907-08 season seems to have been particularly bad. There was no cash for a new strip and the rent was long overdue; eventually the Glasgow Skye Association came to the rescue, as it so frequently did, by donating to the club the entire takings from its spring concert. But by 1912 the secretary was again warning the annual meeting that "we are getting deeper into debt every year" and even hinting that the club might have to be wound up unless "drastic action" were taken. But it never quite came to that; somebody always came to the rescue at the last moment, usually the Glasgow Skye Association.

Training, or failure to train, was the other persistent bone of contention. "The committee hope that next season more attention will be paid by the playing members to training as that is the only way the team can reach a state of efficiency and make a good show in the matches they have to play during the season," the minutes of the 1905 annual meeting record. But by the spring of next year the vice-captain reported that only one member had turned out for the Wednesday evening training session! Next season the players were offered training facilities at Ibrox, where Glasgow-based players from other football teams shared sessions with Rangers players. But even this inducement does not seem to have worked and in successive years the minutes record appeals to the players to smarten up on training. At one point, in 1908, they even contemplated hiring the services of a professional trainer but it was decided that their funds would not permit this.

Few match reports exist from the early days of the Glasgow Skye, especially in northern papers, and those that do are brief, mentioning little more than the score and, occasionally, the team lists. From the number of players who appeared in earlier home Skye teams, it is clear that there was a constant movement of

The successful Glasgow Skye team of 1909 which won the Southern League, while the second team won the Ian Chisolm Cup. Back row. l-r: Alec Macpherson, vice-president; Dr N Macinnes, president; Alec Macinnes; Donald Macintosh. Middle row, l-r: Archibald Macpherson, honorary secretary; D Maclachlan; C Campbell; G F Robertson; A M Wolfenden: D Livingstone; J Macleod. Front row, l-r: John Macdonald; M J Fraser; William Macpherson; John "Kaid" Maclean (captain); J Macqueen; Dr D Mackinnon; J F Macintosh, honorary treasurer.

young men from the island to the city in the years before World War 1. Names like Macqueen and Nicolson, and Mackintosh and Robertson, suggest that both the Braes district and the south end of the island made a large contribution to the ranks of the Glasgow Skye. A profile of the club in the Glasgow Skye Association's diamond jubilee programme in 1931 suggests it was hard going in the early days:-

> As a fighting force the club had a grim up-hill fight at the outset, for at that time the local Glasgow Cowal and Glasgow Caledonians were among the leading teams of the country and few could hope to succeed against them. Glasgow Skye, by dint of perseverance, gained in experience and power, and the day came when they could with some measure of confidence contest the issue with the most formidable of their rivals.

In June 1906 the secretary was instructed to try to arrange a match with Skye in Portree during the Glasgow Fair, "the object being to renew interest in the game in Skye where it is in danger of becoming extinct". Obviously reports of Skye Camanachd's temporary crisis had become much exagerrated by the time they reached Glasgow! Whether this game ever came off is unfortunately not recorded. By December 1907 they had enough confidence to travel to Kingussie to meet the local team in a friendly challenge match, and beat them 6-4. But it must be admitted — as names like Dallas and Cattanach in their ranks make clear — that they had the assistance of a few stars from neighbouring Newtonmore to help them in their task.

"It is with pardonable pride that I have to state that the season just closed has proved the most successful in the short history of the club," the secretary told the annual meeting in June 1909. The success lay in winning the Southern League championship for the first time without losing a single point, and during the campaign twice beating Glasgow Cowal, the dominant city club. Meanwhile the second team had won the Ian Chisholm Cup in the junior competition. In the following season they were second in the league, though they withdrew from the Camanachd Cup since the opening tie, at home in Glasgow against Kyles Athletic, was set for the day after the Skye Association's annual dance — more a matter of realism than of priorities, perhaps!

In 1911 they again emerged as league champions and won it for the third time in 1912, when they also appeared for the first time in the finals of the coveted Celtic Society Cup. Their opponents were Furnace, one of the top teams of the time, with whom they were to have three thrilling tussles for the trophy in successive years. In his annual report for the 1911-12 season, secretary Archie Macpherson was understandably proud and boasted of the club being "a power in the land as regards playing ability" after their Celtic Cup performance:-

John "Kaid" Maclean and John Macdonald cross camans for the camera sometime before World War 1. Clearly a posed shot, the small gaggle of spectators behind the goal suggests it was taken just before the start of a game. Both men were immensely important to the club, both as players and as administrators. Long after he had given up playing John Macdonald was active in the week-to-week management of the club and, with secretary Archie Macpherson, a brother of Duchan and William Macpherson from Braes, usually travelled with the team to all their games in the inter-war years. Despite his enthusiasm for the Glasgow Skye club John Macdonald belonged to the Torridon area of Ross-shire, though his wife belonged to the island.

Paisley having been beaten in the first round, Cowal was next tackled and the result was a draw of two goals each. In the replay they were easily accounted for by four goals to nothing. The Furnace team, who had beaten Kyles in this competition, now met Skye for the first time. After an exhibition of shinty which has not been surpassed in Glasgow for many a day the teams retired with the result — Skye, 4 goals, Furnace, 4 goals, the latter having equalised in the last minute of the game. In the replay Furnace won the Cup, the score being Furnace, 2 goals, Skye 1 goal.

But their moment of triumph came in 1913 when they again faced Furnace in the final, beating them 5-2 and thus winning the Celtic Society Cup for the first time. In 1914 the same two teams met in the final, but this time Furnace were to emerge triumphant.

In these years immediately before the war Glasgow Skye clearly were, as their secretary had claimed, "a power in the land". In his memoirs, the late Lord Bannerman of Kildonan recalled watching them as a child:-

The teams would appear in all kinds of garb with, as a rule but not always, a team jersey. The Skye, I remember, had a kind of Queen's Park-striped jersey and the famous "Kaid" Maclean (named after a general who had seen service in north Africa) playing at full back or in goal wore a sort of velvet rugby cap with a swinging tassel and sometimes long trousers tucked into his football boots. One Saturday at a Kyles v Skye game I saw Donald McCorquodale, whose brother Hugh was "Fingal", the Glasgow reporter of the Oban Times, running along the touchline with a bunch of shinty sticks under his arm. Donald's burden rapidly diminished as the sticks of his team shattered under fierce tackling. There was one little Skye man on the wing, a particular thorn in the flesh of Kyles, who wore a fisherman's cap with a glossy skip. Donald was exhorting his team, and finally exasperated by the success of the little Skye man, shouted in despair to his team, "Will ye no' watch that bloody admiral!"

John "Kaid" Maclean, another son of Tormod Beag and brother of Charles who was among the founders, was far and away the most colourful and flamboyant character in the pre-war GLasgow Skye teams. But by general acclaim the most outstanding player, in ball-playing skills as well as physically, was the towering figure of Hugh Nicolson from Braes, or Uisdean Mor as he was universally known. Then there were people like Donald M Fraser, known to his mates as Doosie, who returned home to Skye as a schoolmaster just before the war, and was a central figure in the great Skye teams of the early 1920s, a time when the island was challenging for top honours. Despite its training difficulties and shoestring budgets the pre-war Glasgow Skye Club was not short on character and talent.

Chapter 7

Back to the fray

The hopes expressed at the Robertson Cup final dinner in March 1907 about "a strong combination" for a bid for the following season's Camanachd Cup were basically realised. On their return to the mainland in the 1907-08 campaign Skye had the satisfaction of beating their old rivals, Beauly, and going on to meet current cup-holders Newtonmore in the semi-final. At that stage the satisfaction may have ebbed a little; an 8-0 result against you tends to have that effect! But from their re-entry into the mainstream of competitive shinty until World War 1 brought the game, and most other sports, to a temporary halt, they acquitted themselves pretty well and had some enjoyment out of it. Each year they entered for either the Camanachd or MacTavish trophies; they brought neither home but they had several tight games either lost or won; they had two or three drubbings they would probably have preferred to forget; and gave a couple which they probably savoured over a gentle dram on the way home.

In their 11 mainland matches in the seven seasons left to them before the war they used a pool of around 40 players, most of them young, probably in their late teens and early twenties when they first made the team. But a nucleus of players appeared in most of the teams during these years. Ewen Macdougall, the Rocais, fisherman from Lotts, was the goalkeeper, and the first to make the dicey stance between the posts his own on a regular basis. In front of him were Donald "Ben" Macdougall, his cousin who worked in the post office and was already seasoned in Skye defences; and Finlay Kemp, tailor and son of a tailor, whose brothers Rory and Willie were frequently to be found holding the centre or among the forwards. Murdo Maclean, Murchadh an Tailleir of Lotts and latterly Achachore, was usually there, and Sandy Mackenzie from Portree. The Murchison name from Bernisdale was to the fore - usually Donald - and Peter and Duncan Graham, brothers from Clachamish of whom Peter was a particularly skilful player. Around that kernel of regulars Macqueens from Braes, Gillies from Edinbane and assorted Macdonalds, Mackinnons and Mackenzies from various districts appeared from time to time.

Their opening match against Beauly took place at Strathcarron on a cold and showery Friday afternoon in January 1908. Despite the weather a large crowd of local enthusiasts turned out to see Skye pile on the pressure for most of the first half and, with a 1-0 half-time lead, sustain the pressure at the start of the second half.

> Gradually, however, Beauly worked up and for fully ten minutes kept up a perfect fusillade on the Skye goal. The goalkeeping of Macdougall was a treat to witness, and time and again he saved what seemed certain hails. Eight minutes from time the Islesmen scored a second hail and were now two up.

Despite a last-minute onslaught by Beauly, that remained the final score, and at the post-match dinner Sergeant Kennedy, the Skye trainer, "frankly admitted that their goalkeeper had saved the game for them." The Beauly president said it was no disgrace to be beaten by the best Skye team so far to appear, and "the most friendly feelings prevailed." Obviously nobody was thoughtless enough to mention stormier occasions in Portree!

In the second round Fort Augustus scratched to Skye, a mixed blessing for the young island team since it brought them — short of match practice at this level — face to face with the current Camanachd champions, Newtonmore. And Newtonmore at the time was in the full flush of its first great period in shinty, being in the middle of a run of nine consecutive appearances in the Camanachd final, four of which they won. Of the hordes of supporters of both sides who crammed the Jubilee Park, Dingwall, on Friday 6 March 1908, few would have given Skye much of a chance. But in the first half the Skye defence played well and held their opponents to 3-0 at half-time, though the second half proved "a doleful one for the men of the Isles."

> The Badenoch men, speedy and accurate, made short work at goal, and scored no less than five points....It was depressing that the game was so one-sided, the efforts of several of the Skyemen being plucky and commendable.

It was particularly galling to lose by such a margin since Skye had, for the first time, brought three players home from Glasgow to bolster their strength — M Grant, J Macdonald and W Armstrong. This had cost the considerable sum of £4 6s, just a tenth of their annual budget in what had been a particularly costly season for the club.

Perhaps this was part of the reason they deserted the Camanachd competition in the 1908-09 season and entered for the less exacting MacTavish trophy, where their youngsters might hope for a better showing. These hopes were dashed in the first round, however, when they met Wester Ross at Dingwall in March 1909 (Wester Ross being a Dingwall-based county team despite the name). According to the *Northern Chronicle* the game "was a keen and strenuous one, played on splendid turf", with Skye showing most of the skill and Wester Ross doing most of the bustling. At half-time the score stood 2-2, but Wester Ross scored the only goal of the second half. It seems to have been a match Skye were unlucky to lose:-

> In hitting, passing, and dribbling, the visitors were undoubtedly the better lot, but they were lamentably weak at shooting for goal. Wester Ross, on the other hand, played a determined game of the rushing order, and, being the heavier team, succeeded in winning.

In 1909-10 Skye returned to the Camanachd competition and in the first round achieved "a splendid victory" over their old rivals, Beauly. It was quite like old times for the supporters who gathered to give the victorious team "a great ovation "when the Glencoe came alongside the pier at Portree. The match took place at Strathcarron on Saturday 8 January 1910 in the teeth of a gale that must have filled Beauly supporters with foreboding!

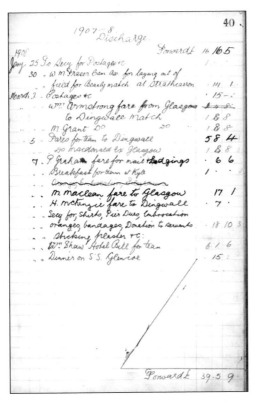

The page from the 1907-08 accounts illustrates the various calls on the club's financial resources. The expensive business of taking players from as far afield as Glasgow could only be justified by results and did not happen every year. Still, even when hard-pressed for cash the team, ever the gentlemen, observed the niceties of making "donations to servants" - a tip for the barman, perhaps? And what are we to make of the ragbag of oranges, embrocation, bandages and sticking plaster as they set off to meet the men from Newtonmore? Was shinty really a rougher, tougher game eighty years ago than it is now?

"Dinner on SS Glencoe - 15s!" Gone, alas, are the days when a whole shinty team could sit down to a sumptuous meal on a MacBrayne's steamer for as little as a shilling a head. The old paddler Glencoe, built in 1846, served for frequent periods on the Portree run in the first three decades of this century, before she was finally scrapped in 1931. She carried the Skye team home on a number of occasions to a triumphant welcome on flag-bedecked Portree pier, and on as many occasions, no doubt, the team's sorrows were drowned in her little saloon! By the time her successor, the Lochnevis, took over in the 1930s Skye teams were finding it more convenient to travel by road to Kyleakin, and take the ferry across to the railhead at Kyle.

S.S. GLENCOE (OVER 85 YEARS OLD) AT KYLE OF LOCHALSH.

The Skye men won the toss, and elected to play with the wind. So strong was the wind, and to such purpose did the islesmen utilise it, that ere half-time they had scored five hails. The wind fell considerably at half-time, and so well did the Skye men play that they scored twice, while Beauly could only find the net once.

A 7-1 victory over the old enemy was certainly worth "a great ovation"; and the northern district final of the competition against Inverness at Strathcarron the following month could easily have gone either way. After a first half of evenly matched play against a strong Inverness defence, Skye were down 1-0 at half-time.

In the second half Inverness made a good start and within ten minutes a second goal was scored by Hepburn. The game now became more exciting and the Skye men were putting in some excellent play. Fraser on the Portree side, with his long shots, was of great advantage to the Portree forwards, who had several byes, and by a smart shot by Graham within ten minutes of time, Skye scored amid the hearty cheers of their supporters. The Inverness forwards afterwards made every effort to score, but the Portree backs Fraser, Kemp and Macdougall were invincible, and when time was called the score stood — Inverness, 2; Skye, 1. The teams dined together and spent a pleasant afternoon. Although the Islesmen lost the game, they took their defeat like good sportsmen.

The 1910-11 season was almost a repeat of the previous one, with Wester Ross rather than Beauly falling foul of an on-form Skye team in the opening match. (In fact, Beauly had been drawn against Skye yet again in the first round but, for some reason, had scratched.) The game took place at Strathcarron on Friday 6 January 1911, with a light dusting of snow on the pitch and visibility impaired by fog! Skye had two goals in the opening minutes and led 3-0 at half-time; Wester Ross rallied in the second half to recover two goals, but fell apart when Skye scored their fourth, to be followed by two more in the final minutes. According to the *Ross-shire Journal* Skye deserved their victory, although the 6-2 scoreline flattered them somewhat:-

Skye hit cleaner in the long grass, they combined well, and they were much faster than their opponents. D Murchison was the best player on the field. He was like a hare for pace. He never slipped and could take the ball from any position. The backs also defended well.

Their success again brought them against Inverness in February in the northern district final, this time on the frost-bound Jubilee Park, Dingwall, but with the same result as the previous season — a 2-1 victory for the mainland side. Skye were back in defence for most of the first half, making only spasmodic attacks on their opponents' goal.

On the other hand, the Inverness forwards pressed with great persistency, and only the magnificent defence put up by the backs and hail-keeper kept down the score. They did register a point, but that was hardly adequate to the difference between the teams. The changing of ends was the signal for vastly improved play on the part of the islanders. Apparently realising that the best means of defence was a strong attack, they followed the ball down to their opponents' end with rushes that kept defenders on their mettle. Time and again the ball was flashed past the outside of each of the posts, and on one occasion in particular, from ten yards out, the ball was lifted yards above the crossbar. The tenure of the game had been completely reversed from that of the first half, and Skye were worthy of a score.

But that score only came after Inverness had gained another goal, and despite a sustained onslaught which pinned the Inverness defence in their own goal area in the closing minutes, Skye's Camanachd Cup ambitions had been brought to a halt by the mainland team for the second successive year.

For the next two years Skye were to meet their familiar opponents, Beauly, in their opening Camanachd Cup games. By this stage the two teams must have been heartily sick of the sight of the other, even if they did drink fulsome toasts to each other after each encounter! Since their return to competitive play Skye had twice dumped Beauly's cup hopes; now the mainland team was to have its revenge. Before the 1911-12 game Beauly tried to have it played at Dingwall rather than Strathcarron "in order to have a fair pitch to play on", but Skye was having none of it; the familiar furrows and molehills of Stratchearron were now home to them. When the teams arrived there on Saturday 3 February 1912 the furrows were under fully two inches of snow, but having travelled so far it was decided to play. In the Beauly goal was the imposing six-foot-six figure of Henry Smith whose renowned long hitting was reckoned to be worth an extra player! In the Skye goal the veteran Billy Ross, who had last played in a Skye strip in 1901, stood in for the unavailable Ewen Macdougall.

At the start play seemed fairly evenly matched but Beauly gradually gained the upper hand and scored within 15 minutes. Another two followed before half-time, and they scored twice in the second half before Murchison managed a consolation goal for Skye in the closing minutes. The *Chronicle's* man-on-the-spot thought Beauly were worthy of their 5-1 win:-

> The victors put up a great defence, in which the long hitting of their goalkeeper was a feature, while their forwards were on their best form, never allowing the Skye backs a moment to settle down. They were superior in every department of the game, and, while the nature of the ground detracted somewhat from the spectacular point of view, their game, all over, was the steadiest they have played for several years. The Skyemen played well, and if their forwards got any chance a different complexion would have been put upon the game. They were up against a better team and the score is a fair indication of the run of play.

Obviously Beauly were leaving their doldrum years, a fact that they were to emphasise by again beating Skye in next year's competition and going on to beat Kyles Athletic 3-1 in the final. The match with Beauly at Pitglassie Farm, Dingwall on Friday 21 March 1913 was, in fact, the semi-final of the cup, though it was also Skye's first game in the competition. It was their third appearance in a Camanachd semi-final since the turn of the century and, as happened on previous occasions, they were helped there by byes and withdrawals. In fact Edinbane, no doubt emboldened by its Robertson Cup success, had entered for the 1912-13 Camanachd Cup and had been drawn against Portree in a north-western district containing only the two teams! Presumably, wiser counsel had persuaded them to withdraw rather than divide the island's resources.

Even so it was a weak Skye team that challenged Beauly that year. The *Inverness Courier* noted that they were "minus several of their players who found it impossible to get away, and their places had to be filled by substitutes." Still, they had the best of the play for the first quarter hour, when 8

Beauly, settling down to their game, got their first goal and followed it with three more before half-time.

> In the second half, similar to the first period, Skye early did the pressing, and on this occasion they were rewarded with the first and only goal secured by them in the match. It resulted from an effective bit of play, which, however, they failed to maintain. Murchison and Graham were putting in some good work, and Kemp at back was playing with great pluck. Beauly had now a complete mastery of the game. Their defence could hardly be said to be tested, and their forwards were playing with great dash.

With such dash, indeed, that they added a further four goals, ending with an 8-1 victory. But the Courier was inclined to be kind to Skye, noting that "in comparison with mainland teams, they lack the benefit accruing from repeated contests. With greater experience and training the present team could put up a good display, and it is to be hoped that they will not lose heart by the heavy total piled up against them on Friday." They did not lose heart but they did exercise a bit of prudence by deciding to spend next season once again tackling the less exacting pastures of the MacTavish competition. It was to be their last season before the holocaust of war engulfed Europe, but they were not to know that at the time.

Their first match was at Strathcarron on Friday 9 January 1914 against the little known Garve Shinty Club. The brief report that remains suggests that "Skye had a splendid team forward, but Garve was considerably handicapped by two of their best players failing to turn up." The score, 7-1 for Skye, bears this out. But whatever the game was like the post-match fraternising seems to have been a success: "A pleasant hour was spent with song and sentiment, both teams parting in true sportsman's style — the best of friends."

In the semi-final of the competition — their last game before the war — it was almost inevitable that they should be drawn against Beauly. Since their first friendly match 19 years earlier the two teams had met seven times in competitive shinty; Skye had won on three of these occasions and were no doubt eager to even the score. They were certainly quick off their mark when the teams met on a farm field at Garve on Friday 6 February 1914.

The lads from the Misty Isle were the first to assert themselves, quickly getting into their stride and helped by a breeze, bearing down on Mackenzie in fine style. Twice in rapid succession they got through the Beauly backs and in two minutes they notched their first hail amid great cheering. For some time after the throw-up they clung round the Beauly hail, and on one occasion missed by a very narrow margin. Gradually, however, Beauly came into the picture, and for the next ten minutes monopolised the play, the ball coming in from the wing in a manner that looked ominous.....D Campbell hit the corner with such precision that it dropped right in front of the Skye uprights and William Maclennan tipped it smartly past the custodian into the net. Time and again Beauly returned to the attack but the defence prevailed until near half-time, when Simon Campbell scored with a swift low shot which gave no chance.....

Within six minutes of the restart Beauly had scored two more, though a late rally by Skye led to a final score of 4-2. It had been a fast and occasionally robust game; "one of the Skyemen was laid out for a time and several of the players received cuts, so uneven was the pitch and so uncertain was the hitting." But the press was full of praise, with Kemp at back and Fraser in the forward line being nothing short of "magnificent", while Mackenzie in goal and Boyd, Macqueen, Nicolson and both Macmillans were deemed worthy of special mention. And the flattering if now rather hackneyed verdict followed them homewards: "The Skye team were undoubtedly the best they have ever sent across to the mainland."

Excluding their first friendly match with Beauly, Skye had played 28 games in the 19 seasons since the first Camanachd Cup competition, all but the two weather-stricken Portree games in 1898 on the mainland. Their modern heirs play as many in a little over a single season. They won the MacTavish Cup once, were semi-finalists in the competition once, and appeared in the semi-finals of the Camanachd Cup three times. Only in two seasons — 1899-1900 and 1906-07 — were they forced to stand idly on the touchline, largely through the blatant unfairness of a system which dictated that all home fixtures were in reality away games, with attendant financial, travel and team availibity difficulties. To return year after year in such circumstances required a particular stamina, a loyalty to the game, and a pride in their island community. Six years were to pass before their next visit to the mainland with camans in hand.

Skye teams, 1908-14

10/01/08 (v Beauly, Camanachd Cup)
Goal,E Macdougall, F Kemp, D Macdougall, M Murchison, M Maclean, J Cumming, H Mackenzie, A Mackenzie, R Kemp, J Macinnes, W Kemp (captain), D Fraser.

07/03/08 (v Newtonmore, Camanachd Cup)
E Macdougall, Grant and Forbes; H Mackenzie, P Grant and D Macdougall; J Macdonald, F Kemp, M Maclean, W Armstrong, D Macintyre and W Kemp (captain)

07/01/10 (v Beauly, Camanachd Cup)
Ewen Macdougall, Finlay Kemp, Donald Macdougall, Harry Mackinnon, Peter Graham, Donald Fraser, Hector Mackenzie, Murdo Maclean, John Macinnes, James Mackinnon, John Macinnes, William Kemp.

07/02/10 (v Inverness, Camanachd Cup)
E Macdougall, D Macdougall, F Kemp, D M Fraser, P Graham, H Mackinnon, H Mackenzie, D Graham, M Maclean, J Macinnes, W Kemp and D Macdougall.

05/02/11 (v Inverness, Camanachd Cup)
E Macdougall, D Macdougall, F Kemp, A Mackenzie, M Stewart, J Stewart, P Graham, D Graham, H Mackinnon, L Gillies, M Maclean and M Murchison.

03/02/12 (v Beauly, Camanachd Cup)
Goal, W Ross; F Kemp, D Macdougall, W Mackenzie,Peter Graham, Donald Murchison, H Mackenzie, A Mackenzie, J Stewart, L Macvicar, Duncan Graham and Murdo Maclean.

21/03/13 (v Beauly, Camanachd Cup)
Goal, E Macdougall (captain); F Kemp, D Macdougall, D Murchison, P Graham, William Macqueen, W Mackenzie, M Maclean, W Fraser, D Macintosh, D Macdonald and George Matheson.

06/02/14 (v Beauly, MacTavish Cup)
Goal, A Mackenzie; F Kemp, P Boyd, C MacMillan, J Murchison, W Macqueen, H Nicolson, M Maclean, M Macintosh, J Macmillan, W Mackenzie and W Fraser.

Islanders of the 4th Cameron Highlanders in the trenches just before the Battle of Festubert, 16 and 17 May 1915. It is very unlikely that any of these troops survived.

"The heaviest fighting fell to the 4th Camerons - men from Skye and the Outer Islands and the Inverness-shire glens - who had a higher proportion of Gaelic speakers than probably any battalion in the service," The Times reported. From the village of Portree alone 26 boys lost their lives, and the losses throughout the rest of the island were proportionate. Among the dead was Billy Ross of Skye Camanachd who had gone to France though exempt beacuse of his age. After the battle Captain Ronald Macdonald also from Portree wrote to his widow: "Every night we patrolled together the long line of trench held by the company until daylight when we used to sit in the shadow of the parapet together, a few Portree boys round us, and have a Gaelic ceilidh, talking over old incidents and looking forward to the future when we would return home....

Also in France, though not with the Camerons, was John "Kaid" Maclean of the Glasgow Skye. He wrote home: "My loss here is the dearth of Gaelic - only met three speakers so far: Donnie Fraser of Beauly (a shinty player), a London Scot and a Cameron Highlander from Barvas, Lewis (Paterson). Yet I sing 'Mo Mhairi Bhoidheach' with great gusto at times. Oidhche mhath leat agus ad fhaicinn gu slan fallain. Leis a h-uile durachd blath do na h-uile Gaidheal coir a tha faisg ort...Good night to you and may I see you alive and well. With every warm wish to every Gael who is near you."

Chapter 8

Challenging for honours

The immediate post-war era was the most exciting and promising time in Skye Camanachd's history since it won the MacTavish trophy in 1898. From the moment competitive shinty began again in the 1919-20 season the club was a serious challenger for major honours, mentioned by the mainland press in the same respectful prose they usually reserved for Kyles or Newtonmore. In the first two seasons after the war Skye fought their way twice to the semi-finals of both the Camanachd Cup and the MacTavish competition, and on one of these occasions won through to the MacTavish final, though the trophy itself eluded them after two tough matches which many thought they should have won. While they achieved such heights relatively rarely during the rest of the 1920s, there were to be some notable encounters with their old rivals from Beauly, and with talented teams from Lovat and Caberfeidh. It was a time that produced some of the most skilful players to appear in Skye colours; they achieved almost mythological stature and old men still talk of their exploits in hushed and reverent tones.

After the agony of war, shinty obviously offered the island a welcome return to normality and a way of healing communal wounds. From August 1919, starting with a credit balance of 9s 4d carried over from 1914, the account book records a bustle of fund-raising activity which had raised the considerable sum of £50 by the end of the year. As the team's successes mounted so also did it's cash demands and by the end of the season the community had raised over £245 to support it, a colossal sum for those days. Some of it came from functions like dances, concerts and sales of work; much more came in small and frequent donations from numerous supporters; and the rest in major donations from people like Peter D Robertson — still at Scorrybreck though he was soon to release the estate for resettlement by crofters — and a new and important benefactor, Duncan MacLeod of Skeabost.

Allied with this impressive burst of behind-the-scenes activity must surely have been some enthusiastic practice games in preparation for the first post-war season, though the press does not record any of them. In fact, the press makes only the briefest mention of Skye's first three competitive matches, probably because of pressure on space as a result of the post-war paper shortage. Their first game, a MacTavish tie against Caberfeidh, took place on the now familiar field at Strathcarron on Thursday 22 January 1920. The Skye team "showed excellent play, especially in front of goal", an assessment fully borne out by a 9-1 scoreline. Three weeks later, on Thursday 12 February, they were back at the same ground to dispose of Kiltarlity (Lovat by another name) 6-1 in the district

73

Major D M Fraser; "the lithe little major..."

Willie Nicolson, Braes; "a tenacious player"

Dan Nicolson, Braes; a Glasgow policeman

Donald Murchison, Bernisdale; "sound as a rock"

Ewen Macdougall, Portree; goalkeeper and fisherman

final of the Camanachd Cup. And next day — to save expense now that they were on the mainland — they travelled to Garve to repeat their 9-1 performance against Strathconon in the second round of the MacTavish competition. These spectacularly high-scoring performances finally earned them the attention of the press and places in the semi-finals of both competitions against the giants from Badenoch, Kingussie and Newtonmore.

The Camanachd tie against Kingussie took place at Pitglassie Farm, Dingwall, on Thursday 4 March 1920 before 1400 spectators, a record crowd at the time for a semi-final. The Skye team, noticeably much lighter than their rivals, was a mixture of pre-war veterans and new talent. Ewen Macdougall, Peter Boyd, D M "Doosie" Fraser (now also known by his war-time rank of Major) and his brother Willie — all from Portree — had played in pre-war Skye teams, as also had Domhnall Chailein, Donald Murchison from Bernisdale. Among the new blood were Jacky Ross (a son of Billy Ross of the early Skye teams) and Vicky Ferguson, from Portree; Neil Murchison, another of the famous Bernisdale shinty brothers; and the Braes contingent, Calum Nicolson, Sam Matheson, Willie "Ruadh" Nicolson and Willie Matheson.

Despite the build-up of anticipation from Skye's earlier performances the game itself, played in a high wind on a rather heavy pitch, was not a classic. Both teams started rather scrappily but by half-time Kingussie had the bulk of the pressure and had established a 3-2 lead. Skye rallied and made several raids on the Kingussie goal at the beginning of the second half but, while the Skye defence and Doosie Fraser in particular came in for praise, the heavier Badenoch side gradually established their superiority and eventually won by a 7-3 margin. All the press critics felt Kingussie deserved to win though perhaps the score flattered them.

> Their skilful combination, clean hitting, and effective placing of the ball were worthy of their reputation. The Skyemen have no reason to be discouraged by their defeat. They have a very promising team and with continued practice they will still further develope. Their weakness in hitting told against them, and their forward line were not properly supported, with the result that they lacked opportunities of showing their paces.

The two matches against Newtonmore to decide who went through to the final of the MacTavish Cup were a very different matter. The first game, at the Jubilee Park, Dingwall, on Thursday 1 April 1920, ended in a 3-3 draw after extra time and earned a glowing, if brief, tribute in the *Ross-shire Journal:-*

> Some brilliant play was witnessed on the part of both teams, and it is questionable if a better match has been seen in the North for some years. Newtonmore if anything combined better, but the Skyemen were nippier on the ball and very clean hitters. They also appeared to last the pace better. If anything Skye deserved to win. The six-foot Hugh Nicolson from the Glasgow Skye was the most conspicuous man on the field. He was the mainstay of the Skye team.

Another *Journal* correspondent was much taken with "the lithe little major (Doosie Fraser, presumably) who with caman and brain so often out-played the

Newtonmore forwards. His anticipation was a treat to see, his hitting almost unerring." Perhaps the feeling that Skye ought to have won came from the suspicion that the ball had found a hole in the net for Newtonmore's first goal!

For the replay at the same venue a fortnight later Uisdean Mor and the legendary Dan Nicolson (a brother of Calum from Braes) were again brought north from the Glasgow Skye at the personal expense of Duncan MacLeod, Skeabost. Colin Murchison, another of the Bernisdale family, and John Maclean, Braes, were the other changes from the Camanachd team that met Kingussie. For the first fifteen minutes the Skye goal was under constant siege before Newtonmore scored from a scrimmage. They got their second goal against the run of play early in the second half and from that moment the game changed according to the *Northern Chronicle*:-

> Notwithstanding this reverse Skye continued to press, and they only got their deserts when they scored. From this point there was only one team in it, and that was not Newtonmore. Amid the greatest excitement, the spectators being mostly supporters of the Skyemen, the men from the Misty Isle continued to press. Shot after shot was sent in, but luck and the goalkeeper defied them. Just on time Cattanach in goal stopped a lightning shot with his club. A second later the Skye players were congratulating the Newtonmore men on their win. Newtonmore won the first half, Skye the second, and a draw would have been a fairer reflex of the game.
>
> Experience was all on the side of Newtonmore, whose tactics, however, in putting the ball into touch during the last 20 minutes of the game were not sportsmanlike

In fact Newtonmore's tactics led to the introduction of a rule against time-wasting in cup games. The *Ross-shire Journal's* man was intrigued by the amount of local support for Skye. Why should this be, he pondered, and came up with answer that it was because the islanders were such good losers: "it is this quality — their sportsmanship — which has won them the partisanship of Ross-shire mainlanders." Even with that compliment the islanders would presumably have preferred not to be losers of any kind, but at least they had achieved enough to nurse real hopes of a major breakthrough next season. They were to come very close to it in both the MacTavish and Camanachd competitions, only to be foiled on both occasions by Kingussie.

Skye started the 1920-21 Camanachd campaign in fine style with a 5-1 victory over Ross County on 26 November 1920. "From the display of caman play which the Skyemen gave on Friday at Dingwall, it is evident that the island players are capable of great things this season," the *Inverness Courier's* correspondent wrote. They proved him right by returning to the Jubilee Park on Christmas morning and whipping an off-form Kiltarlity 8-1 in the second round. The frozen pitch was covered with large pools of water, and were it not for distance and expense the game would never have been played, but still "Skye, who have a capital team, gave a great exhibition of shooting." They returned to Dingwall on Friday 28 January 1921 to meet Beauly in the district final, their first clash since 1914. The pitch, having thawed, was now a sodden morass but even so the game was "fast and exciting", and the Skye forwards, with Doosie Fraser leading them, found the net in fifteen minutes and held that lead at half-time.

> The elements favoured Beauly in the second period, but a rearrangement of the Skye team served to put more cohesion into their play. Major Fraser took up his accustomed position in the back lines, and for a time play was more or less confined to midfield. Beauly took up the running and Simpson had the satisfaction of putting his side on an equality of scores. This success was short-lived. Skye, with their characteristic fighting spirit soon regained the lead. Victor Ferguson, who had been playing a splendid game, shortly afterwards added a third point, and the game ended with the score — Skye, 3; Beauly, 1.

In the semi-final Skye were now to meet a rampant Kingussie, who had just ousted local rivals Newtonmore from the MacTavish competition, and the press were expecting great things. "The Skye team is as clever and dashing as any that

Duncan MacLeod of Skeabost (1876-1950); businessman, philanthropist, and benefactor on a large scale of Skye shinty among many other causes. Duncan MacLeod, one of the eleven children of a Broadford crofting family descended from the MacLeods of Raasay, was reputed to have left Skye with a half-crown in his pocket and returned a millionaire! He laid the foundations of his fortune as an export manager in Glasgow. He afterwards controlled and managed the whisky firm of Bulloch Lade which he sold to the Distillers Co Ltd, and eventually set up the firm of Duncan MacLeod and Co which had an annual turnover of £15m in its heyday. He bought the Skeabost estate from the Macdonald family in 1920 and immediately embarked on experiments to improve agricultural output which would be of benefit to farmers and crofters. As well as establishing an educational trust to help young islanders, Duncan MacLeod was actively involved in An Comunn Gaidhealach, the Glasgow Skye Association, the promotion of piping, and local affairs in Skye. He was for many years chieftain of the Glasgow Skye shinty club, and in 1926 presented the Southern League clubs with a trophy for annual competition - the Skeabost Horn, a replica of Rory Mor's drinking horn in Dunvegan Castle. Without his patronage in the immediate post-war years it is extremely doubtful if Skye Camanachd could have met their heavy commitments on the mainland. On one occasion he is reputed to have even helped Beauly with the expense of travelling to Portree to play in a match from which they would otherwise have scratched!

has ever come from the Misty Isle," the *Courier* wrote two days before the game. "Donald Murchison, the captain, is a resourceful player, as is Major D M Fraser, one of the mainstays of the team." And the press were not disappointed even though Skye left the Dingwall pitch on Thursday 3 March (their fourth visit that season) 4-2 down after extra time. "Had the figures been the other way, few would have grudged victory to the islesmen, who never played better in their history," was the *Courier's* post-match verdict.

So what went wrong? Very little — apart from the Skye forwards' ability to pepper the goal with shots and still fail to get the ball in the net often enough! Kingussie got an early goal but were then pinned back for most of the first half, Ferguson in particular making shreds of the defence but, like his colleagues, failing to score. But their half-time 1-0 deficit did not discourage Skye.

> They resumed in great style and were soon swarming around their opponents' quarters, thirsting for the equalising point. After six minutes play the match was equalised. Skye were now in the ascendant and they smartly put on a second hail, taking the lead. Often did they outwit the strong defence of Kingussie, but failed to reach the net...Ultimately, Kingussie, amid excitement, got the equalising point through Dunbar, and when time was called the match stood a draw — two goals each.

In extra time Kingussie showed the greater stamina and the tired Skye forwards could find no counter to their third and fourth goals. Next day the Skye lads visited Strathconon at the invitation of the local team and took part in a friendly which ended as a 2-2 draw. After their display against Kingussie they were treated like heroes and a dance was held in their honour. On Saturday they returned home after their tiring and certainly costly (over £60) four-day trip to the mainland, with the plaudits of the *Inverness Courier* to assuage any disappointment. "The team have youth and enthusiasm on their side, and can look forward with bright hopes to securing ere long the blue ribbon of Scottish shinty!"

Meanwhile the MacTavish competition demanded attention. Beauly were invited to play the opening tie at Strathcarron but, since there is no record of the the match, they may well have scratched rather than face the journey. In any case Skye met Stratherrick in the semi-final in Dingwall on Thursday 31 March. In a tight game in front of a large crowd, and backed in the first half by a strong wind which fortunately dropped at half-time, Skye won 3-2 — a fair result according to the *Inverness Courier:*-

> The forwards on both sides were well kept in check by the back divisions. This was notably the case with the Stratherrick defence. If anything, Skye were the smarter side and showed evidence of practice and training. Stratherrick were slower in their movements, but put up a splendid fight against their more experienced opponents.

For Skye it must have been a welcome change to have been described as the "more experienced opponents" — a measure of their achievement over the previous two years — and, having so nearly toppled Kingussie in their recent encounter, they must have relished the prospect of revenge in the MacTavish final. Certainly the press were agog about the match. In a preview the *Inverness Courier* forecast it "ought to be about as brilliant" as the recent Camanachd final in which Kingussie had defeated Kyles Athletic. "Never before have Skye been playing as well as now. They gave the champions a great fright at Dingwall. The islesmen are determined to take the trophy to the Island. It goes without saying that Kingussie will leave nothing to chance in their meeting with the Skyemen."

Nor did Skye leave anything to chance. As they trooped onto Seafield Park at the Longman, Inverness, on Saturday 30 April the team was strengthened by three of the Glasgow Skye stars — Dan Nicolson, Uisdean Mor and Colin Murchison, all of them brought north at the personal expense of Duncan MacLeod. There were three sets of brothers in the team; Doosie and Willie Fraser, Dan and Calum Nicolson, and Donald and Colin Murchison. Around 2,000 spectators had gathered in anticipation of a keen tussle and the opening minutes did not disappoint them.

FRIDAY, APRIL 29, 1921.

JCATION

TO-MORROW

MACTAVISH CAMANACHD CUP.

FINAL.

SKYE (First Winners)

Versus

KINGUSSIE

(Six Times Scottish Champions).

AT

SEAFIELD PARK, LONGMAN ROAD,

INVERNESS.

On SATURDAY, 30th April.

Throw-up at 3 p.m.

Admission—One Shilling; Boys, 6d.

CUP will be presented on Field after match.

LASSES

)N

ificated

La

We Distincti siderably attention

FED

Skye gets top billing.

After a splendid run by Kingussie, Skye set out to score, and Victor Ferguson shone in the front rank. Big Nicolson and Murchison were both shaping well, and the Kingussie defence had quite a hot time. The lively work of the Skyemen raised the enthusiasm of their supporters, and C Murchison, by a dexterous shot, scored the first goal for Skye. Not content, the islesmen pressed for more, revelling in smart work, and confining the play to Kingussie's quarters.

But while Colin Murchison and Vicky Ferguson frequently sliced through the Kingussie defence they failed to find the net, and the next goal came from a Kingussie breakaway. After a fairly even first half which saw "some fine caman play" and in which "the Skyemen were the livelier, and their tackling was fearless and sure", the teams turned round with one goal each. Kingussie began the second half with an early goal, and their raids on the Skye defence became more frequent.

> It was an anxious time for Maclean, Major Fraser and Murchison, who were playing steadily against the dashing Badenoch forwards. Some exciting tussles took place near the Kingussie goal, and the Skyemen's play looked worthy of a point. But the Kingussie defence could not be broken, and again Kingussie took up the running....Slowly but surely the Badenoch men began to assert superiority...

Superiority, indeed, to the extent of scoring two further goals, and although the Skye forwards attacked to the final whistle their shooting was off target and they could do nothing to avert a 4-1 defeat. Again the Inverness Courier was kind: "It was a keen, fast contest, in which, for a time, there was not much to choose between the teams....Skye has a fine set of young players, and, if they hold together, the day is not distant when a shinty trophy will find its way to Skye." But already, of course, three of these players — the near veteran Uisdean Mor and the younger Dan Nicolson and Colin Murchison — were based in Glasgow, and, since they played for Glasgow Skye, ineligible for the home team in games other than the MacTavish competition . Before the decade was out more of the young players were to follow them in search of work. The MacTavish final was to be the high point of Skye's fortunes in the 1920s. But of course the team were not to know that as they sat down that evening in the Royal Hotel, Inverness, to share Duncan MacLeod's hospitality and drown their sorrows and drink a hopeful toast to next season. They could at least console themselves that in both competitions that season they had tested the eventual champions, Kingussie — "a team without a peer in shinty at the present time." Meanwhile the *Inverness Courier* gave them an end-of-season pat on the back.

> Perhaps the most striking feature among the senior clubs has been the stride forward which Skye has made. Since the close of the war, caman play has been taken up with zest in the Isle of Mist. Most of the members of the Skye team saw active service, and, if we mistake not, one of the players had no less than nine brothers serving (the Murchisons). Surely a record. Skye has been handicapped for lack of a suitable ground, and by the fact that the players were widely scattered. Hopes are entertained that a suitable field will be secured for the coming season, and that Captain Murchison's team, with the help of Major Fraser, who has acted as secretary, will yet achieve great things. Mr Duncan Macleod of Kinloch, the new proprietor of Skeabost, has been a good friend of the club, and has done much to help its progress during the past season.

Obviously Skye had no reason to be down-hearted and must have looked forward to the next season with keen anticipation.

Skye teams, 1920-21

04/03/20 (v Kingussie, Camanachd Cup)

E Macdougall; D M Fraser, Peter Boyd, J Ross, S Matheson, D Murchison, C Nicolson, W Nicolson, V Ferguson, W Matheson, W Fraser, N Murchison

15/04/20 (v Newtonmore, MacTavish Cup)

J Ross; D M Fraser, D Nicolson, J Maclean, D Murchison, S Matheson, W Nicolson, H Nicolson, V Ferguson, W Matheson, W Fraser, C Murchison.

26/11/20 (v Ross County, Camanachd Cup)

J Ross; S Matheson, D Nicolson, Major D M Fraser, D Murchison, C Murchison, J Maclean, W Nicolson, D J Boyd, W Fraser, P Boyd, V Ferguson

30/04/21 (v Kingussie, MacTavish Cup final) J Ross; Maj D M Fraser, J Maclean, D Nicolson, S Matheson, D Murchison, W Fraser, C Nicolson, D J Boyd, C Murchison, H Nicolson, V Ferguson.

Chapter 9

Home again!

Just before the 1921-22 season started the team had a welcome boost to their morale; the Camanachd Association had finally agreed to right the wrong of a previous generation — Skye were at last to be allowed to play their home games at home! The case for Skye was argued by Doosie Fraser and young Vicky Ferguson at the Association's annual meeting. The club's performance over the past two seasons must have highlighted their anomalous position, and one look at their accounts for these years would have convinced anyone of the unfairness of their treatment. The decision caused panic in Beauly! Drawn against Skye in Portree in the district final of the Camanachd Cup and the second round of the MacTavish competition (if both teams got that far) they held an emergency meeting to discuss fund-raising, and they asked Skye if both games could be played in one visit. Since that didn't happen we can only suppose that Skye were no more inclined to be charitable to Beauly than they were to Skye at the turn of the century!

Friday 28 November 1921 was a gala day in Portree — the first time Skye's home supporters saw their team in action since that disastrous match with Beauly in December 1898. Even the school children were given a half-holiday in honour of such a momentous occasion! Caberfeidh were the visitors in the first round of the Camanachd Cup and Skye did their supporters proud on one of the Home Farm fields. The delighted throng watched the Boyd brothers — Donald John and Roddie — and Neil Murchison rattle three goals in before half-time, and in the second half another two followed for a 5-0 victory for Skye. They could hardly have hoped for a better start to the new season, though the euphoria was to last less than two months. On Thursday 12 January 1922 Beauly travelled to Portree for the first time in 23 years — no doubt with some misgivings in view of their last visit! — to play a MacTavish tie next day. "They were well received by their old opponents," says the brief match report, "and the game was a strenuously and fairly contested one from start to finish. The visitors won by the odd goal in three. From whistle to whistle there were thrills and many pleasing touches of play." But whatever the thrills the reality was that Skye had been ousted from the MacTavish by Beauly — and were now to meet them in the district final of the Camanachd Cup, the new Kirkhill club having scratched from a second round tie at Portree because of the expense.

Beauly were back in Portree a fortnight later for the Camanachd tie. Skye had made a few changes to their team which included three Boyd brothers and the two Frasers, with Andrew Macleod, Bernisdale, as a new name. A fair crowd of supporters watched Skye start with "a nice crisp wind in their favour."

Above: Uisdean Mor Nicolson, star of Skye and
        Glasgow Skye
Right: Calum Nicolson, Braes; farm manager
Lower Right: Jackie Ross, Portree
Below: William Matheson, Braes

The teams went about their task with grim determination. Each recognised that it could not afford to give anything away, and while play was not rough, it was decidedly robust. For a quarter of an hour the exchanges were pretty equal, and at times the Beauly backs were sore pressed. The Skye backs were in good form, and Maclean was steady and sturdy. Time and again he saved his side; a great player without a suspicion of roughness in his work.

Robust was the right word. After a clash with one of the Skye Nicolsons the Beauly centre was carried from the field and Nicolson was also asked to go, not for foul play but to even the numbers as the rules then decreed, and the rest of the game was played with eleven men a side. It upset the rhythm of both teams but shortly afterwards, with a long pass out of a hard-pressed defence, Beauly managed to score and led by that margin at half-time. The Skye supporters fully expected Beauly, with the wind behind them, to rule the second half and they did, in fact, have the ball in the net only to be given offside. Meanwhile the Skye defence stood firm and Doosie Fraser kept feeding the forwards with " the long low shots for which he is famous", and from one of these one of the Boyds scored in the closing seconds of the match. "A draw was a fair reflex of the play," the reporter concluded, "and the replay will be well worth seeing."

And well worth seeing it was, particularly the first half. It took place at Ferry Park, Beauly, on Friday 10 February, and Skye took it seriously enough to travel the previous night to be fresh for a 2.30pm throw-up. The game began at a fast pace, with Skye having an early edge.

They hit cleaner and, keeping their places well, they were several times in dangerous proximity to Forsyth. The Beauly backs did not allow the visiting forwards to settle down, but Vicky Ferguson and Willie Fraser had several good tries. The Beauly forwards were well fed by their halves, but Maclean time and again nullified their efforts and prevented a score. The ball was banged from end to end of the field, and the veteran Murchison seemed always to catch the eye.

But Beauly were the first to score, though Skye, attacking "in fearless fashion", equalised six minutes later, and then took the lead half an hour into the game and held it till half-time. The Skye defence held out robustly against sustained Beauly pressure at the start of the second half but in the twelfth minute the equaliser came, and shortly afterwards Beauly's third goal. Skye, now "either tiring or losing heart", lost a fourth shortly afterwards. Doosie Fraser than got a ball in the eye and, half-blinded and in intense pain, was moved from the defence to centre-forward. Three more Beauly goals followed, one of them — to complete Skye's discomfiture — being a rebound from a Beauly forward's neck from a bye-hit by goalkeeper Boyd! Skye's cup dreams, boosted by a fine first half performance, had collapsed in a second half fiasco.

Still, even fiascos eventually fade from the memory and a 4-3 win over the visiting Glasgow Skye team during the Glasgow Fair fortnight, followed by Duncan MacLeod's hospitality for both teams at Skeabost House, helped set the club up for the approaching 1922-23 campaign. Just as well, perhaps, for Skye could hardly have welcomed the news that their opening games in both the

Camanachd and MacTavish competitions were against Beauly! And still less did Beauly welcome the fact that both were to be played in Portree! The Camanachd tie was played on the morning of Friday 24 November so that Beauly could return home that day. The visitors were "in rampant form" and won 6-3, though the brief report adds that "the islesmen were minus several of their best players."

Beauly returned to Portree a month later, on Wednesday 20 December 1922, for a MacTavish tie with a Skye team with a few changes. Most notably two Portree School pupils were playing — Hume Robertson from Broadford, later to make his mark with Glasgow Skye, and Archie Nicolson from Braes, a brother of Willie Ruadh. The game, again played in the morning, turned out to be "robust and physical", so physical in fact that Donald Murchison, who broke many a Beauly attack that day, was "laid out" for a few minutes! Against the run of play D J Boyd snatched a goal in the first half and, after 20 minutes of fierce Beauly pressure in the second half, his brother, Peter, got the only other goal. Clearly, Skye stole their 2-0 victory. Even the local reporter sympathised with the visitors: "It was hard lines on Beauly to lose after having fully three-fourths of the play, but hails count, and Skye grasped their opportunities."

In the new year, on Wednesday 10 January, Skye met Caberfeidh on a rain-sodden Jubilee Park, Dingwall, in the second round of the competition. The game started fast but slowed as the surface was churned into mud; but Skye led 1-0 at half-time.

> On changing ends it was soon seen which was the better team. The visitors appeared to be able to stand the pace better, and this, coupled with their smartness in front of goal, enabled them to increase their score, and eventually they ran out good winners by 5 goals to 0.....Major Fraser was a host in himself, and he did a large share of the work. Donald Murchison, at back, was as sound as a rock."

But Lovat, still calling themselves Kiltarlity, finally brought Skye's MacTavish run to a halt in the district final at Portree on Friday 16 February 1923 in what seems to have been a tight game. With the wind and incline of the pitch in their favour Lovat led 2-0 at half-time.

> The Skye team in the second half went in for hard pressing on the Kiltarlity goal and D J Boyd, with a fine shot, netted the ball. The pressure was continued and William Nicolson equalised the score. The scrimmage was then shifted to the Skye goal, where byes and corners resulted, with some fine play in between. Ultimately Kiltarlity planted the leather in the net. Final result — Kiltarlity 3, Skye 2.

So between them Beauly and Lovat had scuppered Skye's trophy chances for another season, though after a reasonable run in the MacTavish competition. It was as well that nobody in the Skye team had the gift of prophecy. Otherwise the knowledge that these two teams, either singly or together, were to repeat the performance for the next five seasons, would surely have broken the islanders' spirit! And they were to do it usually in the first round, though usually also by a margin of no more than a single goal.

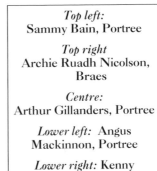

Top left:
Sammy Bain, Portree

Top right
Archie Ruadh Nicolson,
Braes

Centre:
Arthur Gillanders, Portree

Lower left: Angus
Mackinnon, Portree

Lower right: Kenny
Gillanders Portree

The new season began with a Camanachd tie against Beauly in snow-covered Portree four days before Christmas 1923. After a Beauly forward broke his ankle in a hole in the pitch Skye were soon two up, though Beauly had equalised by half-time. In a "strenuous" second half both teams fought for the winner, scored one goal each, and ended with a 3-3 draw. In the replay at Beauly on the first Friday in the new year Doosie Fraser scored for Skye in the opening minute but within three minutes Beauly had equalised. A few minutes later D J Boyd put Skye in the lead again, only to have Beauly draw level before half-time. In the second half Beauly scored twice to emerge 4-2 winners. "Skye had quite as much of the game as the winners, but did not finish so well. That has been the weakness of the islanders for some years. If their forwards were readier to snap up chances they would go far," was the *Courier's* verdict.

A month later, at the beginning of February 1924, Lovat put paid to Skye's MacTavish Cup hopes with a 4-3 victory at Strathpeffer in a match that seems to have gone unreported. In fact Lovat, with a strong team that appeared in the Camanachd final in 1925 and won the MacTavish trophy in 1926 and again in 1928, were to stop Skye in all three seasons, though not without some memorable games. On a sodden Home Farm field at Portree on 23 January 1925 Lovat were to emerge 4-1 winners in a Camanachd tie, though reports suggest the score was hardly a reflection of the play. Skye were fast and aggressive at the start though Lovat scored from a breakaway, but a few minutes later Archie Ruadh Nicolson, still a schoolboy, equalised "with a beautiful long shot from the left wing which gave the Lovat custodian no chance." Lovat's other goals came from goal-mouth scrimmages in this "dour struggle in the mud." The game was to be the last appearance for Skye for the veteran Donald Murchison from Bernisdale. For reasons unknown Skye did not enter the MacTavish competition that season.

On 19 December Lovat were back at Portree for the first game of the 1925-26 season, another Camanachd tie which they won 1-0. There are no press reports of the game but a young secondary pupil at Portree School, Sorley MacLean, was there and he still remembers the occasion vividly. *"Sin far an robh an geam, geam miorbhuileach,"* he recalls,"Now there was a game, a marvellous game....

> Nungan (Angus Mackinnon) was in goal, an excellent goalie, and Doosie Fraser and Domhnall Neill (Donald Macmillan, Braes) were the backs. Uilleam Ruadh (Willie Nicolson, Braes) was right-half, a tenacious player with great stamina, and big Gillies from Inveraray, a banker here and a tall, tall man, was centre-half. Calum Nicolson, my uncle, was left-half; he could be temperamental sometimes, but a marvellous hitter of a ball, and I think that was one of his best games. Uisdean Dhomhnaill Iain Mhoir (Hugh Nicolson, Braes) was centre — that was the year he moved home from Glasgow. The Skye people always said he was their greatest shinty player, though he was past his best when I saw him. He was six foot three and the fastest man in the team and as strong as a horse. And he was so skilful with the stick that he hardly ever sent a ball over the touch-line. Kenny Gillanders, the Glenvarigil gamekeeper's son, was on the right wing and his brother Arthur on the left, and the forwards were Willie Fraser, Peter Boyd and Sammy Bain. That was Sammy's first game for Skye and he was only 18, but when he matured there wasn't a player in Scotland who could match him, at full-back, centre or full-forward."

The second encounter with Lovat that season, in the northern district final of the MacTavish Cup, took place at Castel Leod, Strathpeffer, on 7 January 1926, and again Lovat emerged winners by one goal, with a 4-3 victory. Despite a first half in which "the play was pretty equal" Lovat were two up at half-time, though at the beginning of the second half "Skye exhibited great dash and scored twice within seven minutes." From then on both teams made "strenuous efforts" to gain the upper hand, with Lovat finally successful. After that series of four defeats by Lovat, albeit in tightly fought matches, Skye must have learned with some relief that they were drawn against Beauly in both competitions next season. And Beauly must have been equally relieved that both ties were to be in Strathpeffer.

The Camanachd Cup match was played on 13 January 1927 and mid-way through the first half Skye found themselves 3-0 down in what was turning into a tough tussle. "Charlie Maclennan and Hugh Nicolson in the centre were having a grim struggle," the *Northern Chronicle* reported. "Powerful men both, they showed no great anxiety to get out of each other's way, and their clashes at times savoured of the robust!" Robust or otherwise, Skye had managed to pull two back by half-time, but in an increasingly ill-tempered second half, though they scored one more, they lost another two, giving Beauly a 5-3 victory. For much of the first half of the MacTavish tie a fortnight later Skye seemed to have turned the tables on Beauly and led 2-0 at half-time; but in the second half the greater stamina of the mainland team paid dividends and the final score was 3-2 for Beauly. "Everybody, friend and foe alike, was loud in praise of the sporting spirit of the losers; it must have been disappointing to lose both games in 14 days." said the *Chronicle*. "Skye had several very smart players, and Hugh Nicolson, Bain, Gordon, Gillies and Jack Ross caught the eye oftenest. Mackinnon saved many good shots and his form was equal to anything seen on the same ground for a long time."

The thought of Caberfeidh arriving in Portree for the first Camanachd Cup challenge of the 1927-28 season — instead of either of the terrible twosome of Lovat or Beauly — must have brought a sense of relief to Skye. Unfortunately it was short lived — island weather again decided to go over the top. The Caberfeidh team, having travelled on Friday, awoke in the Portree Hotel on Saturday morning, 26 November 1927, to find their windows lashed by gale-driven rain. Still, it was decided that the game should be played, and a curt report in the *Inverness Courier* tells the rest.

> In fine sporting spirit the Cabers journeyed to Portree, and the match was played in the worst possible weather, and at half-time the visitors were leading by three hails to two. As several of their players were unable to continue the game the Cabers did not go out in the second period. As the match was not finished according to the rules the Cabers would require to again appear at Portree. This the club finds itself unable to do, due in great measure to the great expense of visiting the island a second time. Consequently Skye will enter the second round of the competition.

And inevitably that brought one of the twosome into play — Lovat. Nothing remains of that game, played at Portree on 16 December 1927, except a score-line that reads Skye 1; Lovat 4. And the two teams again met in the district final of the MacTavish Cup at Strathpeffer on 16 February 1928, with Lovat this time gaining a 6-3 win. "The victors deserved to win, but not by so big a margin," the *Northern Chronicle* records. "Skye had out a smart, young team, and if they stick together they should improve with practice and experience." Ah yes, but as the euphoria of the immediate post-war years evaporated, and the lean tail-end of the 1920s gave way to the hungrier 1930s, Skye was finding it increasingly difficult to keep the youngsters together. As they drifted south in search of work, the club became dependent on a dwindling nucleus of veterans, briefly supported by a rapid turn-over of school leavers. Local employment, or the lack of it, was again starting to dictate the fortunes of Skye shinty.

But at the time, of course, there was next season to think about and that brought Beauly to the Home Farm, Portree, for a Camanachd cup tie on 24 November 1928. The capricious island weather had laid another trap for the unwary mainlanders and Skye had a very welcome 5-0 win. The local correspondent of the *Northern Chronicle* highlighted the essential feature of the game.

> Unfortunately, the pitch was the worst on which any important game has ever been played, even in Skye. It sloped considerably and the soil, particularly in front of the hails, had been churned up into a perfect mud bath, which made any spectacular shinty conspicuous by its absence. Often the ball got hidden in the mud, and many a time was only located by the shouts of the spectators. The Skye team suited thir play to the circumstances. They played out to the wings and sent in their shots from an angle. Beauly had as much, if not more, of the play, and they lost because they persisted in planking the leather into the mud in front of the hails, and they beat themselves by persisting in such suicidal tactics.

Enough said, really. This win brought the Skye "mud larks" (as the press dubbed them) to face Caberfeidh at Castle Leod on 13 December, where they made a shaky start against the Strathpeffer onslaught.

> Calum Nicolson and Gillanders were doing their best to stem the tide, and so was the Skye hailkeeper, but Macmaster shook the net just six minutes from the start, and eleven minutes later he added another....Up in the front line Sam Bain and Jagger from the Misty Isle looked eager and active but the home backs gave them no time to steady themselves.

Skye came more into the game in the second half and scored, but Macmaster got his hat-trick, giving his team a 3-1 victory. Kenny Macmaster still remembers the occasion, not so much for any incident in the match, but for the warm welcome that the Strathpeffer lassies gave the Skye players at the post-match dance in their honour! The local heroes were outmatched by the island heroes seemingly. The two teams met again at the Victoria Park, Dingwall, on 3 January 1929 in the district final of the MacTavish Cup when Caberfeidh again won, this time by a 3-2 margin. A good game to watch, was the press verdict, with no great difference between the teams. Except, of course, one vital goal.

On 21 December 1929 Boleskine visited Portree for a Camanachd tie, the first such visit since their fathers had received that weather-beaten 5-1 defeat there in 1898 under the Foyers name. This time they fared better — a 4-4 draw, with no further detail reported. What has passed into Loch Ness-side shinty folk-lore (as retailed by Willie Batchen) is that the team arrived in Portree to find an ample lunch laid for them — with four bottles of whisky on the table! Their manager prudently confiscated them for post-match consumption. Fly men these Skyemen, they still believe down Foyers way. In the return match at Foyers on 3 January 1930 Skye were beaten 3-1, a disappointing reward for a 4am departure by bus from Portree to catch the early train to Inverness with a further bus trip to Foyers, and then the long road home that evening.

Their final foray that season was to Strathpeffer on 17 January 1930 to meet Lovat in the MacTavish Cup. As happened so often in the past few years "both teams were evenly matched", and Skye established an early two goal lead which was reduced to one by half-time. But again victory eluded them.

> In the second period even play also ruled, but Lovat were more dangerous at goal, and secured two hails, thus qualifying for the semi-final stage by 3 hails to 2.

Skye Camanachd played only one more game on the mainland before lapsing into inactivity and withdrawing from all the major shinty competitions. That was on 6 December 1930 in a Camanachd Cup match against Boleskine at Foyers. In a "keenly contested" game they were defeated 4-1. Apart from a single foray in the MacTavish competition in 1939 almost 20 years were to pass before Skye teams began to participate regularly in major competitions again.

Why the rather sudden collapse? The continual drain of young blood south-wards, as witnessed by the number of youngsters who began with Skye and then appeared on the books of the Glasgow Skye, was certainly part of it. The difficul-ties of rasing cash in lean times was another factor. Perhaps also the club failed to nurture up-and-coming talent, as the late Alasdair "Lala" Mackenzie suggest-ed: "The team selectors were a bit old-fashioned and couldn't bear to put an old man out to let young people in, so the youngsters got a bit disillusioned." And Doosie Fraser, a central figure in the club's fortunes for many years and by then playing as important a role in club administration as he had previously played on the field, died suddenly just before the start of the 1931-32 season. Perhaps some combination of these circumstances caused the huge promise of the early 1920s to wither as the decade turned.

Despite the dearth of trophies it had been a memorable decade for Skye shin-ty. Where old men meet who can remember them the talk is still of Uisdean Mor and Doosie Fraser; the merits of the talented Bernisdale Murchisons, or the many Braes Nicolsons, or the three Boyd brothers, sons of a Uist police inspec-tor, are still debated. And despite the temporary demise of Skye Camanachd, shinty in the island did not become moribund. From his island base Angus Mackinnon guested in the Caberfeidh goal for a season; the Bain brothers, Sammy and Johnnie, spent a couple of seasons with Cabers before moving south to join the Glasgow Skye. And the foresight of PD Robertson in establishing a local competition ensured that shinty lived in communities like Bernisdale and Braes, Portree and Tarscavaig, feeding on local rivalry and awaiting the day when a united Skye team would return to the major competitions.

Skye teams, 1922-28

13/01/22 (v Beauly, Camanachd Cup)

R Boyd, D J Boyd, P Boyd, D M Fraser (captain), W Fraser, W Nicolson, V Ferguson, D Murchison, A Macleod, J Maclean, C Nicolson, W Matheson.

10/02/22 (v Beauly, Camanachd Cup)

R Boyd, J Maclean, D M Fraser (captain), J Ross, D Murchison, A Macleod, J Nicolson, C Nicolson, W Nicolson, V Ferguson, W Fraser, D Finlayson.

20/12/22 (v Beauly, MacTavish Cup)

Angus Nicolson, D Murchison, J Maclean, D M Fraser, J Nicolson, F Macinnes, W Nicolson, J Gillies, D J Boyd, H Robertson, P Boyd, Archie Nicolson.

04/01/24 (v Beauly, Camanachd Cup)

Angus Mackinnon, D Murchison, L Murchison, John Maclean, C Nicolson, L Macinnes, J Macinnes, J Ross, D J Boyd, D M Fraser, J Gillies and Ferguson

19/12/25 (v Lovat, Camanachd Cup)

A Mackinnon, D Macmillan, D M Fraser, W Nicolson, J Gillies, C Nicolson, H Nicolson, K Gillanders, W Fraser, P Boyd, S Bain, A Gillanders

07/01/26 (v Lovat, MacTavish Cup)

A Mackinnon, D M Fraser, D Macmillan, W Nicolson, C Nicolson, A Beaton,H Nicolson, A Gillanders, J Fletcher, K Gillanders, D Gordon , J Macdonald

24/11/28 (v Beauly, Camanachd Cup)

A Mackinnon, Jack Ross, J Macdonald, A Macinnes, L Nicolson, K Gillanders, Calum Nicolson, A Buchanan, A Beaton, J Grant, J Jagger and Sam Bain

Chapter 10

Fraser Cup and Skeabost Horn

Some familiar faces gathered in the Christian Institute, Bothwell Street, Glasgow on 7 June 1920 to try to get the Glasgow Skye Camanachd Club on its feet again after the war. Archie Macpherson from Braes, a founder member, was now president; John Macdonald, Torridon, his playing days now over, was an influential voice on its match committee. Both these men, whatever official positions they held, were to figure through the inter-war years, and indeed into the post-World War 2 era, as linchpins in the running of the club. Some of the pre-war stars were present as well, including Uisdean Mor Nicolson, still with some useful years left on the field, and John Kaid Maclean. And there was new blood on the committee, men like Dan Nicolson, a famous defender when the going got tough and equally supportive of the club in an administrative role right to the end. Duncan Macleod of Skeabost was elected chief, a position he was persuaded to hold until 1935 despite his own attempts from time to time to allow the honour go round. But some faces were missing. The minute mentions that the club had suffered "cruel losses to its playing strength" during the war.

Some familiar issues were discussed as well, such as finance and the need for an adequate playing field. On the former, unlike so many pre-war years, the treasurer reported that the club was in a very sound state and outlined the reasons — "increased membership, the liberality of our patrons, and the generosity of the Glasgow Skye Association who have handed us a very substantial sum, the proceeds of their last concert." The Glasgow Skye were to continue supporting the club by giving them the proceeds of the spring "Wee Skye" concert every second year. With frugal management this gave them stability, although there were occasional panics about cash. The matter of the pitch was solved the following year when a conveniently sited field was located "at very favourable terms" at Jura Street, Cardonald. After it was levelled off it served them well until the end of 1928. It was shared, for a small rental, by the Glasgow Inverness-shire team, and it had the great merit of being situated next door to Archie Macpherson's small engineering works which served both teams as dressing-rooms!

But on the field things were not going quite so smoothly. 1920-21 was an "indifferent" season in which they only came third in the Southern League and had to scratch from the district final of the Camanachd Cup because they couldn't raise a team at the last moment. The following season was much better, and in a number of ways, good and bad, set a pattern for the rest of the decade. On the merit side, they won the League and the accompanying Fraser Cup for the sixth time, after a play-off with Blawarthill Argyll. On the debit side Kyles

Athletic put paid to their chances in the Camanachd Cup at the district final stage, and also in the Glasgow Celtic Society Cup, though in the latter Skye were only defeated by the odd goal in extra time of a replay after a 1-1 draw.

It was no great shame to be beaten by Kyles, of course; they were current Scottish champions and indisputably the country's top team in the 1920s, appearing in the Camanachd Cup final seven times during the decade and winning it no less than five times! It was just Glasgow Skye's misfortune, at a time when they were playing well and had some highly-skilled players, that they were trapped in the same district as a team of such overwhelming excellence as Kyles and, on occasion, those lesser Argyll giants of the 1920s, Inveraray. Effectively the way forward in the Camanachd competition and the Celtic Society Cup was blocked, though Skye appeared in the final of the latter a number of times.

In the 1922-23 season, however, Kyles of Bute were the bogeymen. In a game "where science was thrown to the wind for muscular strength" (or so the Skye annual report claims) they won 4-1 in the Camanachd Cup and the Bute men repeated the same score (which "rather flatters the winners," says the Skye report) in the Celtic Cup. To add gall to the wound Glasgow Skye had brought down some home players — much as they supplied Skye with Mactavish Cup players at the time — to strengthen their team for the latter game. This brought a stern rebuke from the treasurer: "The bringing of players from the north devoured much of our savings and I think that in future the club should on no account call for the assistance of home players." But all was not gloom. The club had won the Fraser Cup again (the seventh time), and a second team had been established though once it had to play with only 10 men, and on another occasion John Macdonald, "the father of the team", had to make up their numbers at the last moment!

Socially, as well, it had been a good season. The Glasgow Fair trip home to play Skye had been an outstanding success and, intriguingly, two games were played at Flemington and Port Glasgow against Irish hurling teams. The thought would have gladdened the hearts of the old Skye Land Leaguers who were so thirled to the Irish connection, and it takes no great leap of the imagination to see the hand of the Kaid, inheritor of Tormod Beag's loyalties, in the meetings. It may indeed have been on one of these occasions that he was asked how, as referee, he managed with the rules of the hybrid game. "I just make them up as I go along," replied the irrepressible John! A smoking concert was held in spring to mark Uisdean Mor's forthcoming marriage and to say farewell to young Neil Murchison (the most skilled of all the brothers, some say) who was emigrating to the United States.

Yet the next couple of seasons had the club in a bit of a panic. "I lack the material which gladdens the heart of any secretary of an athletic club, namely an account of victories won and trophies gained," wrote Dan Nicolson in fine style in his report for 1923-24.

There is this year nothing tangible to show our prowess on the shinty field, and the League championship, which in the not distant past we had begun to look upon as our own, has this year been filched from us. True, the virtue lies in the struggle and not in the prize, but I fear that I can only put our defeat down to a waning of that splendid enthusiasm which used to be a feature of the members of our club.

An early post-war Glasgow Skye line-up. Back row, l-r: McCorkindale, Argyll; James Currie, Islay, treasurer; Donald R Macqueen, Braes; Dan Nicolson, Braes; ? ; William Macpherson, Braes; William MacIntosh, Inverness; ? ; Archie Macpherson, Braes, president; John Macdonald, Torridon, match secretary. Middle row, l-r: ? ; Hugh Nicolson, Braes; Douglas Maclean, Inverness; ? . In front: Neil and Colin Murchison, Bernisdale.

In fact a dearth of players was the main problem. The team had to scratch in one League match at the last moment (though still coming second over the season) and the second team became defunct in mid-season. Kyles Athletic again blocked the way to the Camanachd Cup, and Inveraray had defeated them in the Celtic final, though "only when we had been deprived of the effective services of our redoubtable captain, Colin Murchison, through injury." Still, Dan was not down-hearted.

With the revival of industry which is almost upon us, we shall draw more young men from Skye, and I have no doubt but that the Glasgow Skye Camanachd Club will again rise to the pre-eminent position it has, and should always occupy, in the realm of shinty.

But for the forthcoming season he had a rather revolutionary solution for their problems — they should "unite with the home club in order that one strong and efficient team might take the field." This brought a powerful attack from the Kaid, who felt that "it would be deplorable to allow a club like the Glasgow Skye to lose it identity even for one season." After long and occasionally heated discussion Duncan Macleod diplomatically suggested a sub-committee examine the issue. It reported back in September that travel and financial difficulties were against the proposal and it was quietly dropped. But the tantalising thought remains that, if carried, the plan would have placed the talents of the like of Dan, Uisdean Mor and Colin Murchison at the disposal of Skye for the Camanachd Cup....

Next season brought no real relief. Enthusiasm was "at a low ebb" and the second team disappeared as all the players were absorbed by the first team. But with the resourceful John Macdonald scrounging for players ("the survival of the old club is entirely due to the inspiring and capable efforts of our worthy match secretary," say the minutes) they weathered the trough and were actually second in the League. But Kyles Athletic and Inveraray, Scottish champions that year, defeated them in the Camanachd competition and the final of the Celtic Cup respectively. And the news that Uisdean Mor was returning to Skye, following a similar move the previous year by Willie Macpherson, brother of Archie and Duchan of the 1910 Braes team, was a further blow to the playing strength. "Assiduous training is the password to success in this as in any other game," warned Dan Nicolson, "and I would counsel every playing member of the club to spare no effort in this direction next season."

They must have heeded his advice. The 1925-26 season was "one of the most successful seasons in the history of the club, so far as prowess on the field of play is concerned." They took full points in the League, winning the Fraser Cup for the eighth time. They regarded their defeat by Kyles Athletic in the district final of the Camanachd Cup by only one hail scored late in the game as "our best performance of the season," and even if Inveraray did defeat them 3-0 in the Celtic final — well, were Inveraray not current holders of both Celtic and Camanachd cups! But to put the gloss on the season they defeated three city clubs to become first holders of the Skeabost Horn, a new trophy presented by Duncan Macleod. They were to retain it for the next four seasons as well, making it five in a row.

Confidence had returned and morale remained high for the rest of the decade. They again won all their League games in the 1926-27 season, winning the Fraser Cup for the ninth time and thus beating Glasgow Cowal's record number of wins. But Cowal had their revenge by ousting them from the Celtic Cup at an early stage, preventing their appearance in the final for the first time in four years, and inevitably Kyles Athletic won the district final of the Camanachd Cup. And of course there was the considerable consolation of the Skeabost Horn. Alex Robertson, the new secretary, was quite clear where most of the credit lay.

> The success of the team during the past season is in no small measure due to the whole-hearted play of D R Macqueen at centre, particularly his ability as a goalscorer, he having 15 to his credit for the season, this being only two behind the leading scorer, our redoubtable captain, V Ferguson, whose 17 goals stamp him as one of the finest forwards in the game.

Next season they had to be content with the Skeabost Horn, second place in the League, and the fact that for the first time since the war Kyles Athletic

' SHINTY v. HURLING

SCOTLAND BEST IN THRILLING STRUGGLE

SCOTLAND, 2 Goals; IRELAND, 1 Goal.

The visit of a Scottish Shinty team to Croke Park, where they met an Irish hurling team on Saturday, aroused considerable interest. The game was followed with rapt attention by a huge crowd, and at times enthusiasm reached a high pitch. Scotland were victorious after a fast and strenuous, but thoroughly sportsmanlike game.

The last occasion on which a shinty team visited Dublin was in 1897, when the Cowal Shinty Club played the Celtic Hurling Club at Jones's Road. Mr. Michael Cusack, founder and first president of the G.A.A., was referee.

The first change noticeable in the game when compared with our national pastime of hurling was the difference in goal posts and methods of scoring. The "net" is much narrower than the hurling goal, but higher, and points, as in hurling, are not counted. The Irish caman is broader and more useful in overhead play; the shinty stick is capable of greater accuracy on the ground. Handling the ball is not permitted in shinty.

The difference in style was at once apparent. The Irishmen, used to clean, vigorous, open hurling, were somewhat non-plussed at the beginning by the brilliant ground work of their opponents.

The handicap was particularly evident in the forward line, where, with the possible exception of Garret Howard and Gleeson, both Limerick men, the Irish representatives were outplayed.

The Irish crowds were as intrigued by the kilted antics of John "Kaid" Maclean as referee, "picturesquely attired in the Highland tartan" as The Irish Independent has it, as they were by the different code of shinty at the Scotland v Ireland shinty-hurling match at Croke Park, Dublin on 2 August 1924. It was held as part of the International Tailteann Games to mark Eire's recent independence. The Scottish team, which won 2-1, had two Glasgow Skye players, Uisdean Mor Nicolson and D Maclean. A third, Colin Murchison, was on the touchline as a substitute. This may well have been the occasion on which the "Kaid", as ready with rhyme as with a caman, composed "The Shinty Referee" between bouts of seasickness crossing the Irish Sea!

On 29 June 1932 six Glasgow Skye players were included in the Scottish squad which visited Dublin for a similar occasion. The were Alex Finlayson; John Macdonald (An Coileach), Bernisdale; Hume Robertson, Broadford; Kenneth Beaton (Coinneach Mhamaidh), Bernisdale; Donald R Macqueen, Braes; and Victor Ferguson, Portree. "It is pleasing to record that Finlayson and Macdonald were the outstanding players on the Scottish side, the former especially enhancing his reputation by giving a masterful display of goalkeeping," the Glasgow Skye minutes record. Sammy Bain of the Glasgow Skye also captained a Scottish team which played Ireland in Glasgow.

hadn't knocked them out of the Camanachd Cup — Edinburgh University had! To cap this indignity they also lost their Jura Street home, and were peripatetic for a number of years. Still, the rest of the 1920s and the turn of the decade were not bad years even if trophies, apart from the Skeabost Horn, were in short supply. They were usually second in the League — tied with Glasgow Inverness, in fact, in 1930 though they lost the play-off — and usually reached the final of the Celtic Society competition, though the trophy itself, which they had won only in 1913, was as elusive as ever. They were certainly confident enough in 1929 to spurn an invitation to merge with a proposed Glasgow Camanachd Club that would unite the city's shinty talents in an all-out assault on the major trophies.

The Shinty Referee

O sure I'm not sea-faring
But I'll tell you how I felt
When we went o'er to Erin
To meet our brother Celt
Ach, the boat she started tossing
When Dick Cameron said to me
"'Twill be a divil of a crossing
For the Shinty Referee!"

But sure we're all together
From the castle and the plough
The shamrock and the heather
They are intermingled now
Long may they be in harmony
And rivalry prevail
To show the world our flags unfurled
And we are Clann nan Gaidheal.

But that blooming Irish Ocean
Sure she neither ebbs nor flows
She set me right in motion
From my head down to my toes
Till the big and little fishes
Came up in turns to see
And gave their grateful wishes
To the Shinty Referee!

No longer are we troubling
About the grand old game
Since we have seen in Dublin
Both countries play the same
Those camans told of days of old
Of muscle, brawn and brain
So let us strive to keep alive
Our grand old fathers' game.

As for differentiation
I would never ever dream
Agin Ireland as a nation
We had an ideal team
Yet Ireland said about the Kaid.
Our humble Referee
"'Twas such as him with heart and limb
that set old Ireland free!"

John Kaid Maclean

And then, in the 1931-32 season, came the long-awaited breakthrough, in "what has been one of the most successful seasons in the history of the Glasgow Skye Camanachd Club." For the second time they won the Celtic Society Cup, and they did it by achieving the unimaginable — beating the great Kyles Athletic! Hume Robertson's annual report was exultant.

> Playing in the second half of the game minus Donald R Macqueen, who had been removed to hospital following a serious facial injury, we held Kyles Athletic to a one goal draw on a muddy field at Westerlands, and in the replay at Shieldhall beat them by the only goal of the match, thus defeating our famous rivals for the first time in the history of the club.

Add to that the Fraser Cup for winning the Southern League and the Skeabost Horn for a sixth time out of a possible seven, and Glasgow Skye's various cups were surely full to overflowing! Then, of course, there was the reflected glory of having had six of the team's players chosen for the international shinty-hurling match with Ireland. But there was one sad aspect to the season — John Kaid Maclean had been killed in an accident on the West Highland railway line.

Glasgow Skye 1931-32, Celtic Society Cup winners. Back row, l-r: Ian Ross; Charles Wilkinson; Donald Macleod; Ian MacLeod; John F Macintosh; John Nicolson; Alex Mackinnon. Middle row, l-r: William Mackintosh; Archie Macpherson; D B Grant; A Maclean; A Finlayson; A Young; D Grant. Norman Gillies; John Macdonald. Sitting, l-r: K Matheson; J Macdonald; D R Macqueen; K Beaton; D Beaton; V Ferguson: H D Robertson.

But in the next season, unaccountably, the Glasgow Skye blew it all. They were only third in the League, Kyles Athletic beat them in the first round of the Camanachd Cup, Glasgow Mid-Argyll did the same in the semi-final of the Celtic Cup, and the Skeabost Horn went to Glasgow University. To cap it all only one Glasgow Skye player — Sammy Bain — was chosen for the team to meet Ireland in a shinty-hurling match at Shieldhall. But at least he had the distinction of captaining the Scottish team that was narrowly beaten 1-0. The team's performances in the 1933-34 season were marginally better, though none of the trophies were regained. They did, however, create something of a record in playing eight games in the Camanachd Cup and not getting beyond the second round! In the preliminary round they beat Edinburgh University 4-0 after two 3-3 draws. In the first round they drew twice with Glasgow Inverness-shire before defeating them 4-1. And before their 2-1 second round defeat by North Bute they drew 1-1 with them!

Worse was to come. The next two seasons rank with the most dismal in the club's history. In 1934-35 they were second from the foot of the League, regained none of their trophies and were defeated 9-1 at Oban on New Year's Day by Oban Celtic in a new competition between the two clubs for the Kaid Maclean Cup, donated in memory of the player by William MacKintosh, one of the Glasgow Skye vice-presidents. "We have struck a lean period," said Hume Robertson's annual report. "It must not last. Let us put our best foot forward and restore our club to a pre-eminent position in Glasgow and Scottish shinty."

But last it unfortunately did, at least into next season. "Not for many years has a Skye team performed so poorly on the field of play," Hume Robertson wrote. Again they were at the foot of the League, and they made no impact in the other competitions, although the second team won the Ian Chisholm Cup. Worst of all the New Year's Day game at Shieldhall for the Kaid Maclean Cup was "a complete fiasco." Although Oban Celtic and a dozen spectators turned up in atrocious weather, Skye could not field a team. The fixture was subsequently dropped and the trophy brought home to Skye for competition.

There was no way now for Glasgow Skye to go but up, and in the remaining seasons before the war a slow but distinct process of recovery began, with John Macdonald recruiting new players wherever he could find them. One of these was Willie Macpherson from Shieldaig:—

> I used to play in the forward line if they were short. They had a good team at the time but it was difficult to get them all together. People like Nicol Bain — a brother of Sammy, a big, strong half-back — he worked on the Corporation buses and often he couldn't get off duty. There were three brothers from Lochcarron, Beatons — Jimmy and Murdo and Kenny — and they were all fine players. And then big George Cumming, the Caberfeidh full forward, joined us sometime around 1937 or 1938. I think he was the best forward I ever saw play. He'd take the ball from either side and it would leave his stick like a bullet. As soon as I saw him on the field I knew we'd get a couple of goals that day. John Macdonald would sometimes say 'This team should be called Wester Ross — there's only three Skyemen here today!'

By 1938 the secretary was able to report the best season for six years. "Players were more regular in attendance and all round a greater enthusiasm was shown. The advent of the Beaton family into our club has helped us considerably." In that year the team had recovered to third place in the League and reached the final of the Celtic Cup where, though giving "a creditable display", they were defeated by the current Scottish champions, Oban Camanachd. The following season improvement, if any, was marginal and secretary Hume Robertson was again emphasising the need for training and regular attendance. "If our players apply themselves with enthusiastic endeavour there seems no reason why the Glasgow Skye team should not be able to stand comparison with the best," he wrote. But he was not to know that six years of war were to lie between that aspiration and fruition.

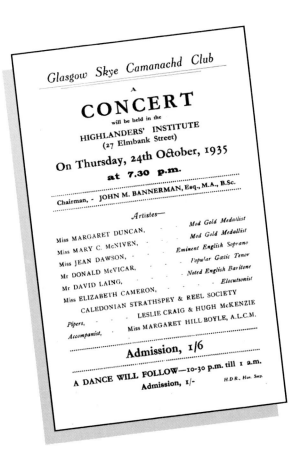

Chapter 11

Braes, Bernisdale, Sleat, Portree....

"Though Skye has not been able this year to enter a team for either the Scottish Camanachd or MacTavish trophies the shinty spirit, it is hoped, is only in a semi-moribund condition, and will yet revive to livelier times." So wrote the Portree correspondent of an Inverness paper in November 1932, almost two years after Skye Camanachd's final game with Boleskine. In fact the shinty spirit was not at all moribund in the island; the Robertson Cup competition saw to that, as did a number of other localised competitions which sprang up in the late 1930s. It is likely that the Robertson competition took place during most of the inter-war years though it is impossible to be sure, since, as a purely local event, it was sparsely reported. Certainly, as early as December 1921 the *Inverness Courier* noted that "shinty is making rapid strides in the island of Skye, and teams are springing up in various districts of the island. A new club has been formed in the district of Strath, and it hoped they may be able to enter the championship next year." No doubt this was largely a grass-roots re-action to the exploits of the Skye team on the mainland in the first two post-war seasons.

Further south, in Sleat, where the tradition of the New Year game was still very much alive in the 1920s, a little informal local league established itself for a few years after the war. It involved townships like Isleornsay, Ferrindonald, Ardvasar, Aird and Tarskavaig. Alan Campbell, Calgary, who played for Ferrindonald can still recall these games. "Everyone from young boys to middle-aged men would play, with home-made sticks made of ash or hazel. Sometimes we played just below the farm steading at Armadale, and other times on a piece of ground beside the Free Church at Knock." The Rev John Macdonald, "a holy terror" according to Alan, and clearly a disciple of Maighstir Ruairidh, was not amused. None of those who played there would meet again to play, he thundered! "As it happens they didn't, " Alan says, "but I don't think it happened the way Mr Macdonald expected. There wasn't any employment here and around 1923 a lot of the boys emigrated to Canada and there wasn't so much shinty after that."

A report of the 1922 Robertson Cup final mentions that the trophy was won by Braes the previous year, but the competition may have restarted as early as the 1919-20 season since Skye Camanachd was already active at that time. In some years as many as half a dozen teams might enter depending on local zeal and circumstances; at various times in the inter-war years Portree, Broadford, Braes, Bernisdale, Portree School and Sleat were represented. The 1922 final, between Portree and Broadford, was held on Portree's public park which was "in miserable condition with melted snow and slush" even in mid-April. On an almost impossible pitch Portree won a 5-1 victory. Who the victors were for the next two years is not known but in 1925 Portree School created a bit of a sensation by defeating Portree in the final, and in 1937 they again won the trophy by beating Sleat.

Against all expectations Broadford got their revenge in December 1926 by beating Portree 2-0. (It may have been an early final that season because of a lack of teams; Braes was not very active in the mid-1920s.) The following November Broadford found themselves back at the Home Farm park in Portree,

Portree School team, Robertson Cup winners 1925. Back row, l-r: Alasdair Robertson, Portree; Calum MacSween, Raasay; Sandy Macdonald, Harris; John Macdonald, Harris. Middle row, l-r: Angus Beaton, Tarscavaig; Tom Fraser, Uist; Hector Mackinnon, Broadford; Archie Nicolson, Braes; John Mackinnon, Harris. Seated: Donald Matheson, Portree; Lachie Boyd, South Uist (captain); John Fletcher, Breakish.

Two of the team, Angus Beaton and Archie Ruadh Nicolson, played for the famous Skye teams of the 1920s as schoolboys. Angus, who subsequently played for Glasgow Skye — "one of the strongest players for his size I've ever seen," according to Sorley Maclean — now lives in his native Tarscavaig, and is probably the sole survivor of the team. While Lachie Boyd and John Fletcher played for Skye occasionally in the 1920s (and Alasdair Robertson in 1939) it was characteristic of Portree School teams that they supplied players to central Scotland rather than to Skye! Most players who passed through Portree School went on to further education or sought employment outwith the island, and thus appeared in the ranks of the university teams for a while, and subsequently with clubs like Glasgow Skye or Edinburgh Camanachd, or indeed, a variety of mainland clubs. It is a rather sad commentary on island education in the early part of the century that it was so heavily geared to an academic export trade rather than to furthering the needs of the local community. Nor were the schools particularly interested in furthering shinty; the Portree School team of 1925 owed as much to the response of its members to Skye's mainland successes as it did to official encouragement within the school. That attitude has, fortunately, changed quite dramatically within Skye schools in the last quarter century.

this time to meet Bernisdale who had last won the Cup some 13 years previously. Bernisdale had already defeated Portree by a decisive 7-2 margin in a previous round.

> The Bernisdale team showed their superiority in the first stage of the game by scoring twice in the first five minutes, although they had lost the toss and were playing against a strong north wind. After the previous night's heavy rain the ground was very treacherous, still both sides showed clean hitting, and a fast game was displayed. The Bernisdale forwards, D Beaton and J Gordon, were quick and deadly in their attacks. At half-time the score was 4-1 for Bernisdale, and during the remaining part of the game they augmented the score 6-1 in their favour. The cup was later on presented to the winning team, represented by their captain, K Beaton, by Major D M Fraser.

With players like Uisdean Mor, Kenny Beaton (Coinneach Mhamaidh), and Donald and Lachie Murchison in their ranks, their victory on that particular day should have caused no great surprise. But, like any other team, Bernisdale also could have their off days, and they did so in spectacular fashion in the Robertson Cup final two years later, in November 1929, at the school playing field in Portree.

> On the previous Saturday Portree defeated Broadford by 6-3 and, as Bernisdale expected to turn out a good team to meet Portree in the final, a keen game was expected. Spectators were disappointed, as the game proved almost a walk-over for Portree, resulting in a victory for the home team of 16 hails to one. In both sides there were very young players. The result does not give any indication of the zeal and determination of Bernisdale, who played a plucky game to the end. In the evening the Robertson Cup was presented to the winners by Major Fraser in the Portree Hotel, after which a smoking concert was enjoyed by the company assembled.

The understated delicacy of the reporting is impressive — almost a walk-over? But not all the participants attended the concert that night. Iain Mor Mairi Shaw, Bernisdale's cheer leader and organiser-in-chief, took his shinty seriously and was in no mood for festivities. As the final whistle blew he stalked from the field and, face red with shame and anger, walked the long miles home to Bernisdale through the watery bogs of the Mointeach Mhor, since he couldn't face the humiliation of meeting a car or a person on the road to whom he might have to admit the score!

In 1930, and again in 1931, the cup was won by Portree, who had an 8-1 victory over Braes in the latter year's final.

> Portree won the toss and the ball quickly found its way into their opponents' territory. At half-time the score was 2-0 in favour of Portree. On change of sides the home team again kept the visitors' goalkeeper on the alert and in constant action. The match ended in a well-deserved victory for Portree of 8 hails to 1. Braes, a newly revived team, from the results of this match are by no means to be considered as players not to be seriously reckoned with, as they played a hard and keen game.

The appearance or otherwise of district teams in the competition from year to year would depend on the supply of young players at home, or even on the presence of an individual with sufficient initiative to organise them. Frequently, players well past the veteran stage would fill any gaps. Given the predominance of Braes and Bernisdale players in the Glasgow Skye team in the 1920s it can well be understood that their home districts might have difficulty raising a team. In Braes, Duncan (Duchan) Macpherson, a brother of Archie of Glasgow Skye fame and himself a member of the first Braes team to win the Robertson Cup in 1910, was usually team organiser in the immediate post-war years. For Portree, the island capital with a slightly larger population at its command, the problems of raising a team were not quite as acute. The Robertson Cup competition continued to prime island shinty throughout the 1930s, even if it attracted little press attention. In November 1932 Braes, obviously recovered from their lean years, beat Sleat in the final at Portree, and the following year were defeated in turn by Portree. The competition generated some fierce rivalries, notably between Portree and Bernisdale, each of which regarded themselves as kingpins of the competition, not a sentiment that would find much favour in Braes!

If players did not turn up for a match, spectators were sometimes pressed into service. John Davidson, Portree, was helping his father build a house in Achachore, when he saw spectators gathering on the Home Farm park for a Saturday afternoon match. "I took an hour off and wandered down to see what was going on, and before I knew where I was a caman was thrust into my hands, and I was told to run over to Creagliath and borrow a pair of tackety boots from Kenny Mackay, and there I was on the field — playing against Bernisdale!" Team colours and strips also tended towards the informal, indeed towards the non-existent on occasions. "I don't think I ever saw Domhnall Chailein or some of the other Bernisdale players strip for a game when I was a kid," Hamish Macintyre recalls. "They would arrive at the field, throw off their jackets, tuck their trouser legs into their stockings, and run onto the pitch swinging the caman. Then they would come off at the end, put on their jackets and walk all the way home without breaking sweat!"

Some of the pitches left a lot to be desired as well, though whether they were any worse than some of the surfaces Skye Camanachd played on in formal competitions must surely be a moot point! "They don't play nowadays in the sort of conditions in which we had to play," says Donald Angy Macleod, Portree. "Good God, they pack up now for a shower of rain! We had to play in muck, furrows, hollows — all sorts of filth, and we weren't trained as they are today. We'd come straight off a fishing boat and straight onto the field. They play a lot better nowadays because the pitches are that much better."

Apart from affecting the quality of modern shinty that improvement in the playing surface has had an impact on the style of play as well. "The style has changed considerably since our young days," the late Alasdair (Lala) Mackenzie recalled. "They play more combined shinty now and use the open space a lot more; they look to find their man better. In the old days there was nothing that got more applause than a long hit — if you could swipe the ball and send it about 200 yards, that got a cheer. But it invariably gave the backs plenty of time to grab it since it was coming towards them in any case."

As the 1920s drew to a close and some of the younger element felt that they weren't getting a fair crack of the whip from the local "shinty establishment" — either of the Portree club or Skye Camanachd — a number of them got together to form the rather grandly named Portree Junior Athletic Club. "Donald Angy and I were involved, and boys like Alasdair Robertson in the Portree Hotel and Jimmy Peacock," Lala explained. "Some of the younger Skye Camanachd players joined us, people like Angus Mackinnon and Sammy and Johnnie Bain, and the Gillanders brothers — and we challenged Skye Camanachd to a match and we beat them! Then we entered for the Robertson Cup and were drawn against Bernisdale. They had Domhnall Chailein and Donald Macmillan, Braes, the Skye full-backs, playing for them and of course we thought the writing was on the wall for us. But there was snow on the ground when we met them in the park behind the school and you couldn't see lines or anything and we beat them 8-2!"

As the 1930s progressed a number of other competitions were introduced which had the effect of once more providing a link between the island and the mainland, though at a much more localised level than the major Camanachd

A Portree Club line-up from the early 1930s. Standing, l-r: Johnnie Bain; Alasdair "Lala" Mackenzie; Norman "Baxter" Beaton; John "Loll" Jagger; Neil "Barney" Macleod; Murdo Maclean, Camustianavaig; Kenny Matheson; John Alec "Reindeer" Nicolson. Kneeling, l-r: Murdo Maclean; Calum Nicolson; Ian "Monty" Munro; John Davidson

competitions. In 1934 the Lochcarron general practitioner, Dr Charles Ferguson, a native of Glendale, Skye, presented the Lochcarron Camanachd Challenge Cup for competition by teams from Skye, Wester Ross and Glenelg, and a number of the Skye teams — including Portree, Portree School, Bernisdale and Sleat — took part at various times. Portree entered for it in both 1935 and 1936, but withdrew in the seasons leading up to the war because of the additional travelling expenses involved. In 1935 Lochcarron defeated them 5-0, while the score the following year was 2-1 in favour of the mainland team. In 1938 Portree School had entered the competition but were defeated 4-0 by Kintail at Portree. The Kaid Maclean Cup, "repatriated" from Glasgow when it became clear that the New Year's Day matches between Glasgow Skye and Oban Celtic were off, was also open to island and neighbouring mainland teams. In February 1939 Bernisdale defeated Lochcarron 2-0 in the final at the Home Farm park in Portree.

The south end of the island had also revived local competitions in the immediate pre-war years, with teams involved from the villages where shinty flourished in the early 1920s, as well as from Broadford and Kyleakin, with occasional visits from teams from Glenelg, Lochalsh and Lochcarron. In the latter end of 1938 the Schools Camanachd Association, again with the backing of Duncan Macleod, Skeabost, had ambitious plans for setting up a schools' league involving the whole of Skye and the adjacent west coast mainland.

With such progressive developments going on in the area it's not too surprising that Skye Camanachd should shake itself out of its decade's slumber and look to the future. It entered a team for the MacTavish competition for the 1938-39 season, and with the aid of a bye, was drawn against Caberfeidh in the district final. The game took place at Blairninich, Strathpeffer, on 14 January 1939, and Skye were to face a 5-1 defeat. No team list was published, but Archie Macdonald, Tarscavaig, then at Portree School, was one of the players, and to the best of his memory the others were:— "Doots" Nicolson, Portree, in goal; Sammy Bain, Portree; Alec MacKillop, Bernisdale; Lachie Murchison, Bernisdale; Neil Macdonald, Tarscavaig; Martin MacInnes, Tarscavaig; Iain Robertson, Broadford; Jimmy Peacock, Portree; Angus Beaton, Tarscavaig; Dan Macdonald, Bernisdale; Frank Coull, Portree.

"Cabers were then a famous team," Archie recalls. "They had a couple of Cummings and Bartletts playing and Tom Mackenzie at centre. We hadn't played together, you see, and Cabers were always together — I think that was one of the main reasons we lost." The only press report of "quite a good game played in a fine sporting spirit" on a frost-bound pitch bears him out.

For a team which had not played together on any previous occasion, the Skyemen gave a creditable display, particularly in the first half, when they put up a grand fight. They created a very favourable impression and did not deserve to be beaten so heavily, although the defence went to pieces in the last 15 minutes, losing three goals. Nicolson in Skye's hail made several fine clearances, and he and Frank Coull refused to waver.

But the revival, welcome as it was, had come rather late in the decade. Before another shinty season opened the holocaust of total war was again unleashed.

An t-Earrach 1937	Spring 1937
Air an raon fhada leathann	On the long wide field
An ear-thuath air Port-righ,	North-east of Portree,
Shuas air cul a' bhaile,	Up behind the village,
Raon mor iomain na Borlainn,	The big Home Farm shinty field,
Sgioba Sgoilearan Phort-righ:	The Portree School team:
Gillean mu shia-diag 's mu sheachd-diag,	Boys about sixteen and seventeen,
Iad uile deante is sgairteil,	All well-made and full of vigour,
Cruadalach agus tapaidh,	Hardy and courageous,
Sgitheanaich, Ratharsairich, agus fear dhiu	From Skye and Raasay, and one,
Leodhasach mor socair laidir.	Big, strong and gentle from Lewis.
Latha o chionn lethchiad bliadhna,	A day fifty years ago,
Latha grianach ciuin,	A calm sunny day,
Gun snaithnean ceotha air a' Chuilthionn	Without a thread of mist on the Cuillins
No air claigeann a' Stoir.	Or on the skull of the Storr.
Ach an diugh ceo eile	But today another mist
Air raon mor na Borlainn,	On the big Home Farm field,
Ceo na lathaichean a dh'fhalbh	Mist of the days that have gone,
Ciar thar na h-oigridh a chaill an oige	Dim over the youth who have lost their youth,
Is ochdnar dhen da-dhiag marbh.	And eight of the twelve dead.
Chaill iad uile an oige	They all lost their youth,
S i'n toiseach mar linn eile,	Which was at first like another generation,
Ach an ceann da bhliadhna	But before two years ended
Borb le cunnartan a' chogaidh,	Barbarous with the dangers of the war,
Le tinneas, leointean agus bas,	Sickness, wounds and death,
A shearg fluraichean na h-abhaist	Which withered the flowers of the customary,
Ged a tharr a' mhor-chuid as.	Though the majority survived.
Am bliadhna tha buidheann eile	This year there is another band
A cheart cho gleusda 'n Sgoil Phort-righ,	Quite as skilled in the School of Portree,
A cheart cho calma ris an sgioba	Quite as hardy as the team
A bha san t-stri air raon na Borlainn	That stood on the Home Farm field,
Mun do bharc an leth-chiad bliadhna	Before the fifty years surged
Air an linn laidir ud de dh'oigridh.	On that strong generation of the young.
Somhairle MacGill-Eain	Sorley MacLean

Sorley Maclean's poem is based on the Robertson Cup final of 1937 when Portree School defeated Sleat to win the trophy for the second time. As a young teacher Sorley played for the school. The school team that day was Alasdair Macleod, Raasay; Willie Lockhart, Portree; Sorley Maclean, Raasay; Alasdair Campbell, Breakish; Willie Reid, Kyleakin; Angus Macdonald, Lewis (living in Arnisort); Murdo Ferguson, Carbost (captain); George Buchanan, Borve; Ruari Mackinnon, Broadford; Donald Gillies, Raasay; Donald John Robertson, Strath, Peter Finlayson, Dunan. Two of them — Alasdair Macleod and Peter Finlayson — were killed in the war.

Chapter 12

Lochcarron .... and a cup

As the servicemen trickled home from another war — one that hadn't hit Skye quite as disastrously as World War 1, though the losses were still severe — camans were howked out of forgotten corners. In the summer of 1946 groups of men would meet on the *"bugha mor"* in Skeabost, or the Home Farm field in Portree, or down by the farm steading at Armadale, and practise skills that had lain dormant for six years. The youngsters of the community, who had little opportunity of seeing shinty during these years, gravitated towards them. The game was coming alive again. The Robertson Cup competition was revived, again proving the foresight of P D Robertson 40 years earlier. Portree, Bernisdale and Tarscavaig entered teams in the latter half of 1946, with the trophy going to the Tarscavaig team. But noticeably absent was a team from Braes, that power-house of Skye shinty in the glory days of the 1920s. Depopulation had taken its toll in that once populous community; the local primary school was closed and the pupils transferred to Portree, and the ageing population could no longer raise a team. Its two outstanding players, the pre-war veteran Murdo Maclean and young Alec Michie, played for Bernisdale. Tarscavaig, which had so much shinty talent immediately before the war that it supplied four players to the Skye team that played Caberfeidh (and it also won the Robertson Cup that year), kept going for another three or four seasons, then it too had to withdraw. "The 1946 team was made up of returned ex-servicemen on demob leave, and when they had to go away in search of jobs the writing was on the wall for us. The population was ageing and we simply couldn't keep a team going any longer," Archie Macdonald recalls.

Portree, Bernisdale and Portree School kept the competition alive for a few years more, before the two former communities had to pool their resources in a common effort to sustain a Skye team. Regular local competition died out around the 1953-54 season and the Robertson Cup, having served island shinty so well over the years, found a final resting place with Bernisdale. But Skye was also involved in a wider competitive field in the immediate post-war years, set-ting out quickly to re-establish the links that had been forged in the 1930s with the adjacent mainland teams. The pool of players for the island team was drawn mainly from the Portree and Bernisdale clubs. Portree supplied veterans like "Monty" Munro and Kenny Matheson (Kenny Dhomhnaill a' Chornair), a younger generation like John Mackenzie (Jonacks), Billy Mackinnon, the brothers Harry and Ewen Mackenzie, Murdo and Angus Nicolson, Murdo Macrae, Alasdair Peacock and Ewen Matheson, and up-and-coming youngsters like Ewen Maclean and Donald Macleod (Corky) from Scorrybreck. From Bernisdale came the veteran Lachie Murchison (Lachie Chailein) and nephew Angus, Charlie Mackenzie and younger brother Alastair, Neillie Campbell, Alec Mackillop, Angus Beaton (Am Buldy), the Macrae (Dotal) brothers John Alec, Donald and Calum, the Maclean (Laban) brothers Cally and Alasdair, Roddy and Alec Nicolson from Borve, and Donald Munro, also from Borve. And many, many more, for most youngsters in that community — aye, and the not-so-young — could handle a caman and were willing to help out, even if they did not play regularly.

The Skye team's affairs were usually organised through the Portree Club, which picked up in 1946 where it had left off in 1939 — with a balance of 9d in the bank, Angus Mackinnon as president and "Monty" Munro as captain. With the support of people like Hamish Macintyre as secretary, Jimmy Peacock as vice-president (followed by John Davidson and Finlay Kemp), and committee members like Harry Bruce, Alasdair "Lala" Mackenzie, Jimmy Dewar, Kenny Matheson, Sammy Bain and Angus Nicolson they steered the club into the 1950s. They began the assault on the mainland in December 1947 by inviting Wester Ross — a one-year experiment in pooling resources by Lochcarron, Kintail and Glenshiel, and Lochalsh, which broke up when they reverted to their local loyalties — to a couple of challenge matches with a Skye team made up equally of Bernisdale and Portree players. The following year it was decided to enter a Skye team for the Sutherland Cup and MacGillivray Junior League competitions, and the pattern was set for the island's competitive efforts for the next decade. Since both competitions were organised initially at district level with successful teams moving on to the national semi-finals and finals, this meant that Skye's shinty efforts were mostly concentrated on the western seaboard.

There were some memorable and enjoyable encounters with the teams from Kintail, Lochalsh and Lochcarron. A close relationship developed, with friendship and keen rivalry going hand in hand (rather like Portree and Bernisdale), particularly with the boys from Jeantown. The Sgitheanaich and the Carrannaich were no strangers to each other, of course. While Lochcarron had concentrated on local Ross-shire competitions in the earlier part of the century when Skye's sights were set on the major trophies, the local people had supported the island teams at Strathcarron. In any case, there had been much contact and a degree of intermarriage between the east coast of Skye and the neighbouring mainland throughout the nineteenth century; they were essentially the same Gaelic people. Not that that prevented disputes. Skye were quick to lodge a protest after a Sutherland Cup match which they lost 7-3 in December 1948, when they measured Lochcarron's pitch, crammed between the street and the sea, and found it short of the regulation length! A replay was ordered which Lochcarron won 5-3; after that the Carrannaich took to measuring the Portree ground and reckon they found it short on occasion!

But Skye had their revenge in the 1949-50 season when they beat both Lochcarron, by 8-2, and Lochalsh to top their section in the Sutherland Cup. The score against Lochalsh in Portree was equally convincing — 7-1, with

Jonacks Mackenzie and Neillie Campbell each scoring three, and Ewen Macqueen getting one — although on this occasion the Skye weather gods almost stopped the tie: "Towards the end of the game visibility was so poor that the ball could hardly be seen at 20 yards, and it has been suggested that matches should be started earlier!" This brought them against Beauly in the quarter-final played at Lochcarron (allegedly a neutral ground though the fact that the Lochcarron ladies plied the Skye team with soup and sandwiches at half-time must surely cast doubt on that!). Skye didn't really expect to win since Beauly had dropped their senior league commitments that season and put all their resources into the junior competitions. But win they did, by 5-4, and they defeated Straths Athletic 6-1 in the semi-final, to win through to a final confrontation with Newtonmore.

That took place at the Ferry Park, Beauly, on Saturday 1 April 1950. Skye were taking no chances. They hired a 20-seater bus from Neil Beaton Ltd for the trip, and stayed overnight in Inverness to be fresh for next day. And next day, against the predictions of most pundits, they were fresh enough to defeat Newtonmore by a 5-4 margin and become junior champions of Scotland for the first time! It was a close game, according to the *Northern Chronicle's* brief account.

> Both teams made a good impression. The lads from Skye made repeated attacks on the Newtonmore back line and soon scored through Mackinnon; Mackenzie got the second. D Maclauchlan scored for Newtonmore but before the end of the half Portree added three more to make a total of five. In the second half Newtonmore had a greater share of the play and managed three more goals. The Skye boys kept their lead of one goal but a draw might have been more favourable.

And a draw it might well have been if it had carried on much longer, according to Billy Mackinnon who, with Neillie Campbell and Angus Macdonald, got Skye's other three goals: "We had most of the play in the first half but Newtonmore put the screw on us in the second half and we hardly saw the ball in the forward line — another few minutes and I'm not saying they wouldn't have equalised. It was a pretty tense time for our supporters as well. I remember "Fiddler" (Jimmy Peacock) throwing his cap in the middle of the field and doing a great song and dance when it was all over!" And so the 1950 team — which had what was arguably Skye's best and most cohesive forward line ever, despite the individual brilliance of earlier players — brought home the island's first shinty trophy in just over 50 years. They had a reasonable run in the same competition the following year as well, being defeated 5-3 at the semi-final stage by Straths Athletic at Castle Leod, Strathpeffer. But in the 1951-52 season, hard-hit by the departure of half their cup-winning squad southwards in the course of their employment, they had to withdraw from that level of competition. Their fall-back was the ever dependable Robertson Cup within the island, and the Kaid Maclean Cup, brought out for competition with the Wester Ross teams on such tourist occasions as Skye Week.

The next three seasons were essentially a period of rebuilding the team, with many players who had reached the veteran stage turning out occasionally to help the remaining nucleus of the 1950 team blood the youngsters, many of the latter still at the schoolboy stage. The difficulty was keeping enough of them employed on the island to give the team an element of stability. Most of the matches in these years were with the neighbouring mainland clubs, and while a number of them were fairly tight, Lochcarron in particular was managing to block Skye's onward progress much as Lovat had done in the mid 1920s. But a lot of the real spirit and character of shinty flowed through these games, with keen rivalry on the field and serious socialising off it! The players of that era still have fond memories of it.

The Sutherland Cup team of 1950. Back row, l-r: Harry Bruce, secretary; Calum Maclean (Cally Laban), Bernisdale; Alasdair Maclean (Alasdair Laban), Bernisdale; John Mackenzie (Jonacks), Portree; Murdo Nicolson (Yochal), Portree; Angus Murchison (Aonghas Dhomhnaill Chailein), Bernisdale; Neillie Campbell, Bernisdale; Donald Macleod (Corky), Portree; Angus Mackinnon (Naongan Dhomhnaill), president. Front row, l-r: Angus Macdonald, Portree; Charlie Mackenzie, Bernisdale; Billy Mackinnon, Portree; Alec Michie, Braes (played for Bernisdale); Ewen Maclean (Eoghainn Iain Eoghainn), Portree.

Shinty "pedigrees" show in this team. Jonacks was a son of Alasdair "Sandy" Mackenzie, captain of the 1907 Portree team and pre-World War 1 Skye player; Angus Murchison was a son of Donald Murchison (Domhnall Chailein), the famous 1920s Skye full-back; Billy Mackinnon is a son of Angus Mackinnon, the 1920s Skye goalkeeper (back row, right) and a grandson of Billy Ross of the 1890s Skye team.

Within a year or so six members of the team were lost to Skye shinty, since they had to leave the island to follow careers — Calum and Alasdair Maclean, Murdo Nicolson, Angus Macdonald, Charlie Mackenzie and Alec Michie.

Even within that limited range of travel, transport could still provide problems for a club that largely depended on the occasional sale of work and, more frequently, dances, for its barely adequate income. (Fortunately, the local people were still as fond of dancing as they were when J A MacCulloch wrote of them at the turn of the century, though the post-war dances were distinctly less formal.) It certainly could not afford to hire Beaton's bus for routine visits to Lochcarron, though occasionally cars might be hired at nominal fees, or, indeed, subsidised by local businessmen who often provided anonymous support to the club. Frequently, Colonel Jock Macdonald, Viewfield, returned from India shortly after the war, would pile the entire team into his ancient Morris van and equally decrepit trailer and transport them to Kyleakin, or sometimes even to Strome. They perched inside, carefully keeping their feet from the gaps in the floorboards, and watched in disbelief as the road flashed by below! Sometimes the Lochcarron players would meet them at Strome Ferry and take them the rest of the way into the village. Donnie Mackinnon remembers one of them giving him a pillion ride on his motor-bike: "He went through every pot-hole on the road, and my goodness there were plenty of them! I was rattled to pieces except for my legs. They were rigid with cramp from gripping the pillion and I could hardly run for the first half hour of the match!"

The return journeys by train sometimes had unexpected results. Hamish Macintyre recalls the occasion when the team took over the guard's van coming back from Strathcarron: "Monty Munro was sitting on top of the big wheel that controlled the brake and one of the boys suddenly grabbed his legs and spun him around and the whole train shuddered to a halt. Half the passengers landed in a heap on the floor!" On field as well, the bizarre could happen. In one game Corky Macleod, a difficult man to ruffle though no shrinking violet, suddenly took it into his head that Lochcarron's Charlie Stewart had been unnecessarily zealous in a tackle, and made to tell him so in a forthright manner. Charlie took off down Lochcarron's long main street with Corky in hot pursuit, waving his caman like a dervish intent on grievous bodily harm! The game came to a halt and players and referee stood in amazement as the pair disappeared round a distant corner. A couple of minutes later Corky re-appeared, having given up the chase, followed by Charlie at a circumspect distance. The game proceeded and the grievance disappeared with the first post-match dram in the Rockvilla!

The diet of local competition was offset occasionally by visits from teams from farther afield to take part in invitation challenge matches. One of the most memorable of these was at Skye Week 1954 when Inverness arrived to play a Lovat-Skye Select for the delight and edification of the many overseas tourists who thronged the island. No doubt the Lovat element in the team owed a lot to Willie Cowie, the former Lovat player and one of shinty's all-time greats, who had settled in Skye a couple of years earlier. Colonel Jock Macdonald was on hand with a microphone to explain the finer points of the game to the tourists. An average shinty score, he told them, might be in the region of 3-2 or 5-3. Within 10 minutes the score was 3-2, by half-time it was 7-5, and it finished 11-10 for

Inverness! As the *Oban Times* summarised it: "There was some excellent stick work , though the goalkeepers were rather overwhelmed."

In the 1955-56 season Skye added the Strathdearn Cup to their competitions, only to find their way blocked once more by Lochcarron, who defeated them 4-1. But the lean years were over and the next season saw them break out of their west coast corral and fight their way to the finals of both the MacGillivray Junior

The incomparable and much-loved Colonel Jock Macdonald of Viewfield. A man of laconic wit, the stories about him are legion and most of them are true. He was a son of Harry Macdonald, Viewfield, founder member of Skye Camanachd, and he was as loyal to the cause of shinty in Skye as his father. He was born in 1889 and as a child in Portree Primary School played the game, though during his secondary education in Fettes College, Edinburgh, he took up rugby, and was once capped for Scotland. Jock followed a career in tea and served in the Indian Army and remained in India for many years. When he and his wife returned to Skye shortly after World War 2 his Gaelic, of which he was immensely proud, was still as fluent as when he left as a young man. He was a devotee of piping and a competent performer, and delighted in wee ceilidhs at Viewfield dedicated to good piping and good whisky with like-minded cronies such as Dugald Macleod, a local joiner, Donnie Mackenzie, Post Office, the Dotair Mor (Dr Alan Macdonald) and others of that ilk. He had a clear memory for childhood incident. Once, on a visit to Mairi Mhor nan Oran's cottage in Skeabost, she hid him from his father under her voluminous, floor-length skirts. *"Bha mi gu tacadh, b'fheudar dhomh nochdadh,"* he said "I almost suffocated, I had to get out!" He was a master of the sardonic one-liner. A diligent attender of local funerals, he once, as an old man, turned to a friend of his own age at the graveside: *"Saoil an fhiach dhuinn a dhol dhachaidh a seo?"* he asked. "Is it really worth our while going home?" Colonel Jock was an active life-long supporter of Skye Camanachd, and in its latter revival from 1969 until his death in 1980, its highly respected chieftain.

League and the Strathdearn Cup. In each case their opponents were Kilmallie, reckoned to be one of Scotland's most exciting young shinty teams at the time, with many of the players "fit and ready for senior competitions." The MacGillivray final took place at the Ferry Park, Beauly, on Saturday 18 May 1957, and the Skye team (as near as the collective memory of the players can get it in the absence of a team list) was:—

Ewen Macqueen, goal; Ewen Maclean; John Macinnes, Willie Macpherson, John Don Mackenzie; David Forsyth, Donald Macleod, Donald Mackinnon; John Mackenzie, John Angus Morrison, Billy Mackinnon, Andrew Macpherson.

Of these, Ewen Maclean, Donald Macleod, John Mackenzie and Billy Mackinnon were in the 1950 Sutherland Cup squad; Ewen Macqueen, Braes, was the regular Skye goalkeeper at the time; John Macinnes from Ballachulish worked in Skye; John Don Mackenzie, Dornie, played for them for a season; Donnie Mackinnon, brother of Billy and grandson of Billy Ross, was a first team regular from early in the decade; the brothers Willie and Andrew Macpherson, Torvaig, and John Angus Morrison, Bernisdale were the young intake; and David Forsyth, of the same age group, and another grandson of Billy Ross, played most of his shinty out of Skye for a number of teams throughout Scotland. But the game was not to be a repeat of their 1950 triumph, though Skye, according to the *Northern Chronicle* gave a much better account of themselves than the 6-1 score against them suggests.

> The first half produced fast end-to-end play with both defences kept active by fine forward raids. The goalkeepers were in top form and half an hour had gone before Kilmallie scored the first goal through Burnett. Skye broke through after some grand combination between Billy Mackinnon and John Mackenzie and the latter scored to make it one each.

Thereafter Kilmallie gradually got on top, scoring a further two goals in the first half and three in the second, when Skye's recent lack of match play told and Kilmallie dictated the run of the game. Even so, the reporter had some kind things to say about the islanders' performance: "Skye had some players well up to senior standard. Their goalkeeper was the hero of the game, with Forsyth, Mackenzie and Mackinnon showing up well outfield."

Skye's chance for revenge was to come a fortnight later, on Saturday 1 June, in their first appearance in the final of the Strathdearn Cup, a competition in which they appeared for only the second time. What is more they had the ground advantage, since Kilmallie had generously agreed to play in Portree, the first time a major final had ever been held on the island. Because of injuries sustained in the previous match and the unavailability of some players the Skye line-up was different and read:—

Ewen Macqueen, goal; Murdo Mackay, Lochcarron; John Macinnes, Willie Macpherson; Ewen Maclean; Jock Mackenzie, Lochcarron, Tom Mackay, Lochcarron, Donald Mackinnon; John Mackenzie, John Angus Morrison, Willie Cowie, Billy Mackinnon.

When need arose Lochcarron players sometimes guested for Skye in competitions in which their own team were not involved, as indeed did Skye players for Lochcarron. Willie Cowie, long debarred from playing for Skye until his reinstatement from senior to junior status came through, was eligible for the Strathdearn competition. *The Northern Chronicle* had no doubts about the success of the tie.

> This was a grand game from start to finish. Kilmallie opened on the attack, showing no ill effects of the long journey from Lochaber, and held the initiative through the first half, to lead 3-1 at the interval. In the second period the Skyemen seemed to last the pace better and, if anything, had the better of the exchanges. They reduced the Kilmallie lead to 3-2 and amidst great excitement, pressed hard for an equalising goal.

UP TO SENIOR GRADE

> MacIntyre, in the visitors' goal, was in luck when a Cowie shot rocketed off the upright. Cowie, on best Lovat form, was playing a grand game and had previously scored both the Skye goals. Ten minutes from time Kilmallie made sure with a fourth goal by Burns. The first three were scored in opportunist style by MacVarish. Both sides can be pleased with their showing, which was well up to senior standard. Kilmallie must have the biggest choice of up-and-coming youngsters in the game, judging by recent displays.

NO WEAK LINK

> On Saturday they had no weak link, with outstanding displays by Ferguson, MacVarish, Bruce, and schoolboys Burnett and C Macdonald. The latter finished as strongly as any on the field. The Skye goalkeeper, E MacQueen, was in brilliant form, ably supported by MacPherson and MacLean at backs. At centre field D Mackinnon played a great game — fast and strong on the tackle, his long hitting was a treat to watch. T Mackay was a stuffy centre, with Willie Cowie — crafty as ever — the best forward on the field.

CUP PRESENTATION

> The Cup was presented to the Kilmallie captain on the field by General Harry Macdonald, Portree. The visiting team and officials were then hospitably entertained by the Skye club before setting out on the long journey home. Altogether, this was a most successful and enjoyable day, reflected in the best ever Strathdearn final 'gate' of well over £30.

> Well done, Skye and Kilmallie!

Next season, 1957-58, Lochcarron again put paid to Skye's hopes of a favourable run in both the Strathdearn Cup and the MacGillivray League, but Skye won through to the final of the Sutherland Cup to find that again their opponents were to be Kilmallie. At Beauly in April 1958 Skye's hopes soared when Willie Cowie scored in extra time with the tie at 2-2, but Kilmallie equalised in the closing minutes. In the following week's replay at the same venue Kilmallie won 4-2. But the islanders did not come home entirely trophyless. On the return bus journey John Mackenzie discovered that a rather antique chamber pot, "won" from the Lovat Arms Hotel, had been planted in his bag. Deadpan as ever, Jonacks suggested it might make a suitable receptacle from which to quaff the team's supply of medicinal whisky and made to suit the action to the word when the culprit hastily intervened and confessed that he wasn't quite sure that the pot had been adequately sanitised! The medicine was drunk from medicine glasses and the pot is now probably growing flowers somewhere in Skye.

During Skye Week 1957 Beauly visited Portree as guests at a challenge match with a bus-load of accompanying supporters, some 60 years after the same idea had failed for the lack of a charter steamer. In excellent weather there was "a fast and furious shinty match" which ended in a 4-4 draw. "It was a very sporting gesture on the part of Beauly to come so far to give Skye the practice they need," the local reporter wrote laconically. Presumably nobody mentioned tottering goalposts or winter storms, for next year Beauly were again Skye Week guests and in a "hard-hitting, fast, exciting game" on which the sun again shone, forced a 3-2 victory. In 1959 Skye got as far as the semi-final of the MacGillivray League, where they were defeated 4-3 by Glenurquhart in an extremely tight match which saw a last minute goal by John Angus Morrison disallowed. On such margins are cups won and lost.

But an era was ending for the island team. The men who had served them so well through the 1950s — Jonacks, the Mackinnon brothers, Ewen Macqueen,

A Skye Week line-up from the late 1950s. Back row, l-r: Jimmy Peacock, committee member; John Mackenzie (Jonacks); Willie Macpherson (Uilleam Duchan); Ewen Macqueen, goalkeeper; Donald Macleod (Corky); Andrew Macpherson (Andy Duchan); John Don Mackenzie (Kinlochshiel — guesting); Ian Macdougall (Rocais); Col Jock Macdonald, chieftain. Front row, l-r: Ewen Maclean; Willie Cowie; Donald Mackinnon; John Macinnes; Donald Neil Murchison.

Again some shinty genealogies can be traced. Willie and Andy Macpherson are sons of Duncan (Duchan) Macpherson of the 1910 Braes team; another brother, Kenny, also played and is a referee; three other brothers, Alasdair, Neil and Allan, played mostly for university and Glasgow teams. Ian Macdougall (Rocais) is a son of Ewen Macdougall, Skye 'keeper from 1908 until immediately after World War 1. Donald Mackinnon is a son of Angus Mackinnon, 1920s Skye 'keeper, and a grandson of Billy Ross. Donald Neil Murchison is a son of Lachie Chailein, the youngest of the Murchison brothers from Bernisdale.

Ewen Maclean, the ever-dependable Donald Munro, Angus Murchison — were coming to the stage of hanging up their camans. Willie Cowie, doyen of forwards, was to die tragically young. Corky was to soldier on, lending experience to a younger generation. The senior members of that generation (senior by a very small margin of years) — the Macpherson brothers, Sammy Gordon, Colin Murchison, Ian Macdougall, newly returned from National Service — were to nurse slightly younger lads towards new challenges. They included boys like Hugh and Alistair Clark, Peter and Ally Ruadh Mackinnon, John Matheson, Aldy Macdougall, Calum Beaton and others. Some were to stay and some were to leave the island, as already had two of the promising youngsters of the 1958 squad — John Jagger, whose father played around 1930, and Duncan "Tee" Macdonald. Meanwhile Jonacks Mackenzie, a man of few words and steadfast loyalties, and a player of class with a deceptively lazy, loping stride, was to shoulder the administrative burden with very little behind-the-scenes support. In other words, the team was going through another transitional stage.

Lachie Chailein, youngest of the famous Murchison brothers from Bernisdale. Donald was Skye's full-back in the 1920s teams, while Colin and Neil, who emigrated to the United States at an early age, played mostly for Glasgow Skye. Another brother, Aidean, was also reckoned to be a fine player. Lachie started to play for Bernisdale and Skye in the mid-1920s and still turned out for Bernisdale in the post-war revival. A small, neat figure, he would dash down the left wing, cap down over his brows and trousers tucked into his stockings, whirling the caman in one hand. He frequently dribbled and occasionally hit one-handed as well.

The half-acre or so of croft in front of Lachie's house was sacred to shinty. Although it would have provided useful tillage, no spade or plough was ever allowed near it. On it Lachie trained not only his own family but generations of children from the surrounding crofting townships. He would take them from a very early age and spend endless hours teaching them the art of the caman. For his services to shinty in the island Lachie was honoured by Skye Camanachd as chieftain.

Ian Macleod, Torgorm (1889-1970). a brother of Duncan Macleod, Skeabost, and a life-long shinty enthusiast. In the 1930s he had Isleornsay and Duisdale Hotels in Sleat and, with Dr Campbell, did much to promote shinty there. The development of local competitions in the district in the immediate pre-war years owes a great deal to their influence. After the war he had Torgorm farm in the Black Isle, near Conon Bridge, and later moved to the Kingsmills Hotel in Inverness. Whenever the Skye team played in the area during the lean post-war years, when club finances were at a low ebb, he would invariably appear on the touchline, and often treated the team to a meal and hospitality after the match. For his services to shinty Ian Macleod was elected Chief of the Camanachd Association in 1966, the only Skyeman so honoured, although both Archie Macpherson and Hume Robertson of the Glasgow Skye Camanachd Club, and more recently John Willie Campbell, held office as presidents. A number of people connected with Skye Camanachd, including Duncan Macleod, Skeabost, and P D Robertson, Scorrybreck, were vice-presidents of the Association.

In the early 1960s they were again penned into their west coast enclave, struggling to overcome the wiles of Kintail, Kinlochshiel and Lochcarron. Again, the rivalry was keen and the post-match crack was keener, but it was not the road to trophies. Then, in the 1962-63 season, came another breakthrough. They managed to beat Kinlochshiel 3-2 in the first round of the Sutherland Cup and pushed their way through to a meeting with Glenurquhart in the semi-final. There they faltered, losing 3-1 at the Lochcarron ground in April 1963. The possibility of a further surge forward next season was real enough, though some of the key players were now Glasgow-based and would have to travel long distances to games. But the burden of organisational and financial back-up was now resting on too few shoulders and on too narrow a base and in 1964 the club slowed to a gentle halt. It was not moribund; the pulse of life was still there, not far under the surface, and in 1969 it surfaced with renewed vigour, and with more sustained effect than it had achieved at any stage in its previous history.

Chapter 13

Farewell to 'The Skye'

The members of the Glasgow Skye club met in 1946 to pick up the discussion where they had left it in 1938 — in exactly the same building, the Highlanders' Institute at 27 Elmbank Street, and on exactly the same date, 4 October. The gentlemen who ran the committee were nothing if not sticklers for continuity, and the little matter of Hitler's war and a seven-year interval were not to be allowed to alter that. Mr Charles Wilkinson, president, was in the chair as he had been in 1938, and Hume Robertson, secretary, was busy taking notes, as he had done ever since 1931 and as he would continue to do for a number of years yet. There were other familiar names as well. Archie Macpherson and John Macdonald were there among the honorary presidents and, more significantly for the running of the club, both of them were on the match committee as well, along with Alex Nicolson. Clearly they intended to continue the active role they had played in club affairs since before the previous war! One notable name was missing, that of Dan Nicolson, Dan Shomhairle Mhoir from Braes. But he was to return in a couple of years and play the same sort of role for the next decade, indeed until the club quietly lapsed to its death in 1961.

The war was hardly mentioned at the meeting, apart from a thank you to Archie Macpherson for looking after all the club's equipment for the past seven years. The minute of 1938 annual meeting was approved, it was noted that they had a credit balance of £39 15s 4d in the bank, and it was on with preparations for the forthcoming season. It was agreed to enter for the Camanachd Cup, the Celtic Cup, the Skeabost Horn and the Ian Chisholm Cup if all these competitions were held. And held they were, or most of them, though Glasgow Skye did none too well in them as next year's annual report revealed: "Our first game in the Southern League competition gave us a resounding victory over Glasgow University and hopes for a very successful season ran high. However, these hopes were not to be realised for out of the four league games we played, we only won two and lost two, finishing second equal with Inverness-shire to Edinburgh Camanachd who had a point more."

In fact, because of the severe spring of 1947, with snow and frost gripping the country from January until the end of April, the shinty season was curtailed. A failure to get new camans until what season there was had finished didn't help either, and the team failed to get through the first rounds of both the Camanachd and Celtic competitions, as well as the new MacAulay Cup, and the Skeabost Horn was not played for. The only bright spot amongst this gloom was that three of the club's players — George Cumming, Sammy Bain and Lachie

Macrae — had been chosen to play for a Glasgow Select against Edinburgh in a half-hour exhibition match, part of an intercity sports gymkhana at Hampden Park. Sammy hadn't been able to play but George scored the only goal of the match against an Edinburgh Select in which his brother, Sandy, was playing.

But if camans were allowed to grace the Hampden turf, not so the hallowed sward at Ibrox. Through the good offices of Rangers chairman Bill Struth, a personal friend of Archie Macpherson's, the Skye players were invited to join the assorted footballers from out-of-town teams who trained with Rangers. "They all trooped up the first night with their clubs but I knew damn fine they wouldn't get them on the pitch, and they didn't! Training meant lapping and running up and down the terracing." George Cumming recalls. "Next week me and one other chap were the only ones who bothered to appear!" The irrepressible George was one of a number of pre-war Glasgow Skye players who turned up to launch their post-war campaign. In fact he played for them until 1957, when he was 47, and even then he was persuaded back for his goal-getting talent the following year for a MacAulay cup semi-final. After all, he had once scored all eight goals for them in an 8-4 defeat of Mid-Argyll, equalling his own Scottish record in a Caberfeidh v Fort Augustus game. "I wasna too bad in the MacAulay game either — I scored three but they let in six at the other end!" he says.

Among other pre-war veterans back again were John Macdonald, Bernisdale (An Coileach) and Willie Macpherson, Shieldaig, who took over from him in goal for a spell when he stopped playing. "John wouldna go into goal in the hit-about before the game until I went half-way up the park!" says George Cumming. "He was an awfy character, Johnnie... he'd stand no nonsense, the same fellow ..." Around that time, and into the early 1950s, the last major intake of players from Skye was arriving in the city, some of them having seen war service. It was the generation that included John A Macdonald (Jake), Lachie Robertson, Farquhar Macintosh, Bobby Sutherland and Donald Kelly; slightly later they were joined by Alisdair Michie, Calum Maclean (Cally Laban) and Murdo Nicolson from the 1950 Skye team, and by Roddy Nicolson, a nephew of Uisdean Mor who played for Bernisdale and Skye immediately after the war, but hadn't made the Sutherland final team because National Service intervened.

"By the time I got there Angus Greenshields, whose mother came from Skye was captain, and the organisation revolved round people like Dan Nicolson who was secretary and treasurer, and Alex Nicolson, a lecturer at Jordanhill, and Willie Lamont, who did a lot of the organising. Calum Robertson was our link with the Glasgow Skye Association and helped with a lot of the fund-raising, as did Donald Grant, the schoolmaster from Sleat," Roddy Nicolson recalls.

At the annual meeting in September 1948 Hume Robertson was able to report that "the past season has been one of the most successful in the history of the club and certainly the busiest. Players were regular and enthusiastic so that substantially the same team could be fielded week after week." The team topped the five-club Southern League, winning the Fraser Cup yet again, and in the

Camanachd Cup they got as far as the semi-final before Ballachulish stopped their successful run by inflicting a 5-1 defeat. In the Celtic Society competition they followed a confident route to the final but there, unfortunately, "we suffered the biggest defeat in the history of the club when Oban Celtic, playing splendid shinty, beat a very poor Skye team by 10 goals to nil." A good run in the MacAulay Cup was halted in the semi-final with a 6-1 defeat by the then other Oban team, Oban Camanachd. But at least the Skeabost Horn was retained to put beside the Fraser Cup; and perhaps the real success of the season had been to beat their old rivals Glasgow Mid-Argyll in every single competition! On the final page of the minute book, so diligently kept since the inaugural meeting in October 1903, Hume Robertson records: "We look forward with enthusiasm to the coming season. With keen determination let the players see that the highest traditions of the Glasgow Skye Camanachd Club are nobly upheld!"

But despite the sentiment there were leaner years ahead for the Glasgow Skye. For most of the 1950s Mid-Argyll put their decisive stamp on the Southern League in much the same way as Glasgow Skye itself had done in the years after World War 1. This was no doubt to the great chagrin of John Macdonald, Torridon, who was no lover of the Argyll club. At one association meeting when it was airing a grievance against Glasgow Skye he stood up and declared: "Condemnation by Mid-Argyll is praise indeed!" There was difficulty in getting promised players to turn up in time and touchline arguments ensued as the team tried to delay starts until some much needed star arrived. Sometimes they had to take the field with men missing. On one memorable occasion Skye were two men short. A man was left in the dressing-room to hurry on the latecomers should they appear, but meanwhile Dan Nicolson started stripping to meet the emergency; at 64 he relished setting up a record as the oldest man ever to play for Glasgow Skye. Then the dressing-room watchman appeared with a veteran volunteer goalkeeper in tow — Willie Lamont, who was two months older than Dan! To cap it all, he was an ex-Mid-Argyll player.

It was too easy to blame the players for lack of commitment, as some touchline pundits tended to do. "You've got to remember that Saturday was a normal working day for many of them at that time. A lot of them were shift-workers and many of them gave up good overtime sometimes to play," Cally Maclean recalls. The number of players who received urgent telegrams to attend family funerals in Skye on Saturdays was quite remarkable! Glasgow transport officials and Clyde Trust foremen, where Skyemen were employed in fair numbers, must surely have wondered sometimes about this endless supply of elderly relatives who seemed to have a propensity for requiring Saturday burials.

By the late 1950s the number of recruits from Skye to the team was dropping off noticeably. "There simply wasn't the same number of islanders coming to Glasgow as formerly," Roddy Nicolson says. "Work around the Clyde shipyards and docks was going into decline, and jobs were appearing at home, so they stayed. I can recall very few Skye people joining us — Norman Macleod, perhaps, and Alistair Mackenzie and Archie Fraser, and David Forsyth for a while and that was about it. We were increasingly dependent on players from Argyll and Inverness and other mainland centres." And good players they were, many of them, and the club in its final days was grateful to them. But inevitably the identity of Glasgow Skye was affected. While it had always avoided extreme insularity what reason had it to exist unless its predominant identity reflected its name?

On the shinty field it once more got as far as the finals of the Celtic Society Cup in 1954, and won the Skeabost Horn for the last time in 1956. And in season 1957-58 Cally Maclean became the last captain of a Glasgow Skye team to accept a major award when the team topped the League and won the Fraser Cup for the last time. In 1961 the club was allowed to expire gently. In a changing world it had run out of steam and out of any particular reason to exist any longer under that particular name. But many people still remember it with affection. It gave good service to its community for almost sixty years.

GLASGOW SKYE CAMANACHD CLUB

MEMBERSHIP CARD

SEASON 1959 — 1960

NAME *R. Nicolson*

Colours   MAROON — WHITE

Membership Fee . . 5/-

One of the last membership cards to be issued before Glasgow Skye Camanachd Club expired from natural causes.

And one of the last Glasgow Skye teams: back, l - r, William Lamont, Angus Greenshields, Donald Skinner, Alan Douglas, Sam Macdonald, Murdo Cameron, Dan Nicolson; Front, ?, Malcolm McKellar, Roddy Nicolson, Norman Macleod, Peter Finlayson, Bob Purcell.

Chapter 14

A fitting finale

On Friday evenings and Saturday mornings during the shinty season in the mid to late 1970s motorists on the mainland highways to Skye were often waved down by three or four or five youngsters thumbing a lift. A goodly part of the Skye Camanachd team was on its way home for that weekend's MacGillivray League tie! The club, running on a bank overdraft at the time, couldn't afford to pay their expenses; and the lads, young apprentices and students in Inverness and other mainland centres, were on meagre wages or skimpy grants, and couldn't afford to use public transport. But such was their commitment to the club that they were willing to devote their weekends to endless hours of waiting by roadsides in all kinds of weather to play for their home team, spurning the chance of playing for teams nearer at hand. The hitch-hikers usually were Donnie Martin, Donnie "Digg" Macdonald, Alistair Cruickshank and Ewen "Yogi" Grant — all names that had a significant role at various times in building a Skye team that could challenge the top teams on the mainland. "If these boys hadn't been willing to do that Skye Camanachd would have gone to the wall," says Donnie Mackinnon, team manager at the time.

Interestingly, all of them got their first taste of shinty in primary school, although not all of them took to this particular sporting diet initially. Donnie Martin was at Kilmuir Primary school around 1967, when the Skye primaries received an issue of camans to try and encourage the game among the kids. "The first day we got them we smashed the ball through the classroom window and the camans were locked away after that!" he recalls. Other schools were more enlightened though many of the boys rapidly lost interest because of a lack of positive guidance. "I simply didn't know what shinty was at the time," says Donnie Digg, a fact that shouldn't be too surprising since Skye Camanachd were then in abeyance, and in any case Staffin, though still an intensely Gaelic community, didn't have the same sort of local shinty-playing tradition that Bernisdale had.

Their real introduction to the game began when they became secondary pupils in Portree High School. "We put our names down for football and rugby but somehow or other we landed up doing shinty," Donnie Martin recalls. "It was quite a while afterwards that we worked out what happened — it was all due to D R Macdonald. Somehow all the members of his Gaelic classes ended up doing shinty!" Through his activities in the school, Donald R Macdonald was to be one of the major seminal influences over Skye Camanachd's fortunes over the next twenty years. A North Uist man, DR, as he is familiarly known, was a pupil at Portree School in the 1950s, but became actively involved in shinty during his university days in Glasgow. When he returned to Portree in 1965 as head of the Gaelic department he started coaching shinty in the school with the help of Colonel Jock Macdonald and Jonacks Mackenzie. When Friday afternoon was designated an "activities" period, shinty coaching intensified and children from outside Portree were given an opportunity to join in. The next step, with the help of one or two enthusiastic ex-players, was to introduce coaching for the primary children outwith school hours, and a new generation of Skye Camanachd's future stars was established.

Skye and Newtonmore line up for the camera before the Thomas Ferguson Memorial Cup match of 1972. Newtonmore won by 6-3. Skye team — back row, l-r: Rory Bain, Hugh Clark, Colin Murchison, John Mackenzie, Sammy Gordon, Willie Macpherson, Andy Macpherson, D R Macdonald. Front row, l-r: Kenny Macpherson, Ewen Grant, Calum Beaton, Alistair Mackinnon, Richard Stoddart, Alisdair Morrison, Ian Macdougall. Referee, G Y Slater, Oban. Newtonmore team — back row, l-r: Rab Ritchie, K Smith, H Chisholm, B Kirk, D Cheyne, B Stewart, I Macgregor. Front row, l-r: J Campbell, W Macbean, J Fraser, I Bain, G Fraser.

The Thomas Ferguson Cup is played for by invitation every year in memory of Thomas Ferguson, a member of Skye Camanachd, who was killed in a road accident in 1971. His was one of a number of tragic accidental deaths which have hit the club in fairly recent years. Others were Angus Murchison, John Matheson, Iain Nicolson and George Michie, the latter a young player of exceptional promise.

Meanwhile, the club had shaken itself out of hibernation. On 2 September 1969 it reconstituted itself with Colonel Jock as president and Duncan MacIntyre, a shinty enthusiast and local police inspector at the time, as chairman, and immediately set about fund-raising for the the forthcoming season. They entered for the usual competitions, the MacGillivray Junior League, the Sutherland Cup and the Strathdearn Cup. "The meeting closed with a feeling of optimism regarding the future of shinty in Skye," the minutes record. That feeling was justified for the club was now firmly set on a progressive course that was eventually to lead to that elusive and much cherished trophy, the Camanachd Cup.

MacGillivray League team, 1973. Back row, l-r: Peter Mackinnon, Ally "Ruadh" Mackinnon, Calum Beaton, John Angus Morrison, Alistair Morrison, Donald "Digg" Macdonald, Alistair Cruickshank, D R Macdonald. Front row, l-r: Ewen "Yogi" Grant, Donald Martin, John Murchison, Ian Macdougall, Hugh Clark, Colin Murchison.

The teams of the early 1970s were built round a nucleus of experienced players who had first worn the Skye colours in the late 1950s, with Donnie Macleod, a veteran of the immediate post-war era, in goal, a position later taken over by John Angus Morrison. The others included Willie and Andy Macpherson, Peter and Alasdair Mackinnon, the Beaton brothers, Calum and Alasdair, D R Macdonald, Hugh Clark, Sammy Gordon and Ian Macdougall. Ian actually first played for Skye against Lochcarron in 1954 — on the day before his fourteenth birthday! But he missed out on much of the period in the late 1950s when Skye were making their mark by his absence from the island through work and National Service. He probably holds a unique record among Portree players — in what turned out to be his last shinty match, in 1982, he played for Bernisdale! "I got a bad knock in that game for my trouble — it probably serves me right," he says. Like Peter Mackinnon, and Willie and Andy Macpherson, he frequently guested for Lochcarron in Skye's idle patch after 1963, as indeed Ewen Maclean, Billy Mackinnon, John Mackenzie and Donnie Macleod had done during Skye's blank season in the early 1950s.

As they gained experience the youngsters being trained in Portree School were gradually blended in with the established players. The first of them to arrive was probably John "Bodach" Mackenzie in 1972, and by the following year Donnie Digg, Alistair Cruickshank, Yogi Grant, Donald Martin and John Murchison were making first-team appearances while still in school. Skye Camanachd was beginning to find its feet again. In 1971 the team reached the final of the Sutherland Cup, only to be beaten 2-0 by Ballachulish at Inverness. At the 1972 annual meeting "general satisfaction was expressed at the performance of the team in the previous season. Though no silver-ware had come to Skye yet, the team had one of the best overall performances in the North to its credit." Indeed, such was the confidence that in 1971 the club had entered the

For much of the 1970s Ewen Morrison was the team's regular driver to away games. For a period of three years, during a particularly lean financial patch for the club, he refused to submit a bill to them. Ewen belonged to Druimuie, just outside Portree, where his family were crofters for many generations. Travelling with him was an education and entertainment wrapped up in one. He had a fund of local history and Gaelic anecdote which he was more than happy to recount, and an equally large repertoire of Gaelic songs which he liked to sing as he drove along. His son, Alistair, played for Skye during this period.

Stars in the making — the Portree Primary School team which won the MacKay Cup in 1974, their first inter-school trophy. Back row, l-r: Stewart Macpherson, Cally Maclean, Donnie Murchison, Iain Morrison, Willie Cowie, Marcus Barnes, Neil Macleod. Front row, l-r: Kenny Campbell, Alasdair Grant, Duncan Macpherson, Duncan Macdougall, Andrew Murchison.

The Portree High School team which won the MacBean Cup in 1974. Back row, l-r: D R Macdonald, Dougie Macpherson, Donnie "Digg" Macdonald, Alasdair Cruickshank, Iain Macpherson, Calum Matheson, Donnie Martin, Alasdair Nicolson, David Macleod. Front row, John Norman Macleod, Calum Macaskill, Angus Nicolson, John Macfarlane, John Finlayson, Iain Nicolson, Kenny Mackay. Subsequent school teams won this trophy in 1976 and 1976-84, the last six being a record number of consecutive victories.

MacGillivray Senior League, the first time it had played at this level since its 1939 Mactavish Cup game, though many of the 1950s teams were thought at the the time to be of senior standard.

In 1974 Skye's Irish connections were renewed when the team was invited to take part in a shinty-hurling match at the Pan-Celtic Festival in Killarney. In many ways it was a memorable affair but in others less so; for instance, nobody seems to remember the score, but everybody still has vivid memories of the Irish post-match hospitality! Their Irish hosts took some of the team to visit a rather plush lakeside hotel largely peopled by excessively rich American tourists. The team members, clearly in high spirits and hopefully in good voice, staged an impromptu ceilidh. "The Americans were so taken with our Gaelic songs that they bought all our drink and tried to persuade us to stay for a couple of nights to entertain them," Ian Macdougall recalls wistfully, "They promised to pay all our expenses." This was the famous occasion on which Jimmy Dewar tried to persuade Colonel Jock to desert his favourite Scotch tipple and in a spirit of Celtic fraternity try an Irish whiskey instead, only to have the Colonel dismiss the latter as: "Adder's piss!" But things of more lasting importance to Skye shinty happened that year as well. Two teams from Portree School brought back the first shinty silverware to reach the island's shores for many years, by winning the two most important trophies in school shinty, the MacKay Cup for primary schools and the MacBean Cup for senior schools — an excellent omen for the future.

The 1976-77 season proved to be a turning point in the fortunes of the club. The second team won the John MacRae Cup, the MacGillivray League Division Three championship, after beating Kincraig 3-2 in an exciting play-off that ran to extra time. It was not one of the major trophies, certainly, but nonetheless welcome in an island that had been starved of any trophies for so long. *The West Highland Free Press* commented:—

> It was the first time for 27 years that the captain of a senior Skye shinty team had collected a trophy. Since the Sutherland Cup win of 1950 Skye's senior players have competed in many finals, but managed to lose all of them. Willie Macpherson and team-mate Iain Macdougall are only two of that host of Skyemen with an attractive display of runners-up medals.

By now the team management system had been streamlined, with D R Macdonald as manager of the second team and Donnie Mackinnon as manager of the first team, replacing a selection committee system that had proved too unwieldy. They were to be ably helped by John Nicolson — John the Caley — whose back-room support down the years has meant a lot to the club. The new managers decided that it would be to the long-term benefit of the club if some of the mature first team members should play in the second team to bring on the youngsters, most of them still in school, thus also giving some of the more advanced second team players a run with the first team. It was realised that in the short term this policy might affect the standard of the first team and so it proved. In 1976 they dropped into the second division, gained promotion for 1978-79, dropped again and finally regained first division status in 1982.

But if 1979 brought the disappointment of relegation it also brought the triumph of a cup victory. After 29 years the Sutherland Cup was again destined for Skye. In a performance "marked more by character and determination than by smooth-flowing shinty" they beat Kyles Athletic 3-2 in Fort William on 12 May.

Skye Camanachd has been fortunate with its sponsors and patrons down the years. They have been an important element in the survival of the club since its distance from the main shinty centres against whose teams it has to play means it has to carry an immense burden of expenses. While travel and communications have become faster and easier over the years, that burden has grown no less because of the greater number of games now played by the team in league and cup competitions. The supportive role played by Duncan Macleod, Skeabost, in the years immediately after World War 1 has been carried out for the last 15 years or so by PBCS - Portree Building & Contracting Services. The company was founded and developed by the Macfarlane brothers, Ian and Neil John, seen here with a 1970s Camanachd squad. The family's business activities go back to a small carrier's business conducted by their father, Davy Macfarlane. He is seen here near the pier in Portree in pre-war days with the Ford half-ton truck with which he used to deliver goods from the evening steamer or the weekly Glasgow cargo boats to the Portree shops. Local children used to vie with each other to have a ride on "Davy's lorry" and help him on his rounds.

Not that too many of their supporters would have cared to bet on the final outcome at half-time when the score stood at 1-1. After dominating the early part of the first half and gaining the lead with a Calum Murchison goal after 20 minutes, Skye were losing their grip on the game when Kyles equalised just before half-time. Then Kyles rocked them with another goal two minutes after the restart. But Skye then mounted a series of attacks which pinned Kyles in their own half, though their goal came from a hit-in near the corner flag.

> Calum Murchison picked the ball up and without waiting for most of his attack to arrive or for the Kyles defence to settle, he hit it long and high to the far post, where a solitary Jock Macfarlane was waiting to scramble it over the line. But Skye's lack of finishing power delayed the killer blow until the last six or seven minutes, when a strong run by Donnie Martin down the middle of the park ended with the ball spinning to the feet of Willie Cowie 15 yards out. Cowie wasted no time in hitting it inches the right side of the Kyles' keeper's right-hand post. The team and support, in recognition of what was unmistakably a winning goal, allowed themselves a lengthy celebration.

And after waiting 29 years who could blame them? From then on it was to be a famine to feast scenario as far as that particular competition was concerned. In the next nine years they were to win the Sutherland Cup a further three times.

Sutherland Cup winners 1979. Back row, l-r, Donald Mackinnon (team manager), Duncan Campbell, Willie Cumming, Kenny Mackinnon Willie Cowie, Alistair Morrison, George Michie, John Mackenzie, Donnie Macdonald (captain), Ian Macdoiugall, Ian "Dowal" Macleod, Calum Beaton, Ewen Grant. Front row, l-r, Ross Cowie, Donald Martin, Jock Macfarlane, Peter Murchison, Calum Murchison.

Their next final outing was against Glasgow University at Oban two years later, in 1981, Skye having had the rare satisfaction of beating Kingussie 8-0 in the quarter-finals, and Lochaber 5-1 in the semi-finals. The Skye support was out in force for the game but, as the *West Highland Free Press* remarked, "there were a lot people around with divided loyalties, for no fewer than nine of the university pool were Skyemen while two others hail from Kyle!" That in itself was surely a remarkable tribute to the success of Portree School's coaching policy. Most of the early part of the game was spent in the university's half of the field but without any scoring, then, on the half-hour mark, Skye got a break.

> Bodach Mackenzie cracked in a speculative shot from the halfway line, and as soon as the ball left his caman young Duncan Macpherson was starting his run on goal; the students' keeper, Ian Gillies (also from Portree) could only chest the ball down and Macpherson was onto it in a flash to ram it into the net. A beautifully taken goal. And within five minutes Skye were two up. Again the move started with a through ball which was picked up by Calum Murchison; due to the close marking of Macdonald, however, Murchison was unable to get a shot in so he pushed the ball into the path of Duncan Macdougall for the youngster to score easily. Skye were really beginning to turn on the style now, and three minutes later they scored number three. This time it was Calum Murchison's turn — he moved out from goal to find himself a bit of space,and smacked in a perfectly hit ball which keeper Gillies had no hope of stopping. So Skye finished the first half already looking like champions.

And they emerged in the end as champions, to the tune of 3-1 in fact, though had the issue been judged purely on their second half performance they would hardly have merited it. Glasgow University had all the pressure, and only some wild shooting and an excellent performance by Dowal Macleod in the Skye goal prevented higher scoring.

Sutherland Cup team, 1981. Back row, l-r, Ian Macdougall (committee), Cally Maclean, Ronnie Macpherson, Willie Cowie, Donald Martin, John Mackenzie, George Michie, Ian "Dowal" Macleod, Calum Murchison, Doinnie Macdonald, John Angus Morrison (manager). Front row, l-r, Neil Maclean, Alistair Morrison, Robbie Macdougall (mascot), Ewen Grant (captain), Peter Murchison, Duncan Macdougall, Duncan Macpherson, Duncan Martin.

Sutherland Cup winners 1985. Back row, l-r, Calum Murchison, Ally "Stenscholl" Macdonald, Calum Macdonald, Donald Martin, Calum "Colombo" Nicolson, Ross Cowie (team manager), Ally "Digg" Macdonald, Alistair Morrison. Front row, l-r, Neil Maclean, Donald "Horace" Ross, Angie Murchusion, Willie Mackinnon, Willie Mackenzie (captain), John "Slippy" Finlayson, Alistair Macinnes, John Mackenzie.

Sutherland Cup winners, 1988. Back row, l-r, Ally Grant, John Mackenzie, Ewen "Crossal" Mackinnon, Donald "Donje" Macleod, Calum "Colombo" Nicolson, Wilklie Cowie, Angus Nicolson, James Stephenson. Front row, l-r, John Macrae, Murdo Gordon, Donald Martin (manager), Ross Cowie (captain), Angie Murchison, Keith Mackenzie (mascot), Ally "Digg" Macdonald, Neil Maclean.

Skye's two other Sutherland Cup victories — both by their second teams, whereas the first teams had played in the earlier finals — were both against Strachur, winning by a 2-1 margin in the 1985 final at Inveraray, and by 7-2 in 1988 at Strathpeffer. In the latter game Skye found themselves two down in 25 minutes though Angie Murchison brought one back before half-time and had another disallowed. But within ten minutes of the start of the second half Skye were one ahead through two goals by Ally Macdonald and Ally Grant.

> Once they got in front, Skye never looked like losing. More pressure led to a penalty which Willie Cowie converted in fine style, and a minute later John Macrae continued the spectacular display with a drive from almost 30 yards. Angie Murchison went on to make it six with a fine solo effort, and Skye looked on the point of running up a cricket score. An eye injury to Ross Cowie failed to disrupt their rhythm, and Cowie was replaced by Neil Maclean. John Macrae went on to complete the scoring in the 79th minute, walking the ball home after a goalmouth melee. On a day when Skye had no real weaknesses once they found the way to the net, there was no question about who was the man of the match — Willie Cowie, who stamped his authority on every inch of the beautifully-prepared Castle Leod pitch.

In between their last two Sutherland Cup successes Skye had also finally managed to get their name on the Strathdearn Cup, but the really big one, shinty's premier trophy, the Camanachd Cup, was still as elusive as ever. There were moments in the 1980s, as Skye consolidated their position in the first division, when their supporters dared hope: "Surely this season..." — but always the early season promise came to nothing by the end of it. They were also in a challenging position for the league championship on a couple of occasions, but that too had come to nothing. The name of Kingussie was writ large on the league competitions of the decade, and in the Camanachd competition Kingussie and that other famous Badenoch name, Newtonmore, shared the honours. It was almost sacrilege to believe it could be otherwise. Yet suddenly in 1990 Skye broke through. Why? The week before the final Ian McCormack, editor of the *West Highland Free Press* came up with this answer:—

> Much of the credit for dragging the team into the front ranks of shinty must undoubtedly go to manager Ross Cowie. At the club AGM last year, when he was asked to take on the responsibility, he made it clear he would accept only on certain conditions. The key one of these was: if players didn't train regularly, they couldn't expect a place in the team. It's a condition Cowie stuck to unwaveringly, and one to which the players responded positively.

That training certainly paid off on the road to the final, which was no easy one. Having dismissed Lovat 4-1 in the first round Skye defeated Kingussie 3-1 in the second. In the semi-final they met tough opposition from Fort William before securing a 4-2 victory in extra time. Now they were to meet that other giant of Badenoch shinty, Newtonmore, with their formidable record of Camanachd Cup performances — they had appeared in the final 46 times and won it no less than 28 times. Even in one of their more indifferent years the thought of confronting them on such a stage was an awesome one, made no less awesome in the weeks before the match by the high level of media interest and the heightened expectations created by the hype. The combination of a romantic and famous island, and a shinty team which was well known and yet so starved of trophies down the years, was irresistible. Whatever happened, history was to be made.

As the spectators crowded onto An Aird in Fort William on the afternoon of Saturday 2 June 1990, it rapidly became clear that the *West Highland Free Press's* famous cartoon prediction of a deserted island had come true. Among the thousands who massed the touchline in bright sunshine Gaelic voices were predominant and the atmosphere was electric. In the opening spell Skye had the

Skye was not short of support at the 1990 Camanachd Cup final as Chris of the West Highland Free Press so memorably records. The "Good luck" card from old rivals Lovat (courtesy Walter Cumming and Duncan Maclennan) may refer to an incident when a Skye goalkeeper is alleged to have made a midnight raid on the larder in a Portree hotel and guzzled a delicious steak pie, not realising that dog food had been substituted for the meat! Having stopped smoking, the same goalkeeper was known to beg cigarettes from the goal judge at moments of stress. There may also be an implication that Skye pitches haven't improved much since last century.

On the perfect surface of the Skye ground, the dogged, health-conscious fitness fanatic, "Bodach" Mackenzie clears and removes his goal area, temporarily blinding David Michie of Lovat.

best opportunities and within 18 minutes Willie Cowie had the ball in the net, only to have the goal disallowed. But now Skye were beginning to take control of the game, as Duncan MacLennan reported for the *Inverness Courier*.

> The Skye forward combination was now beginning to take shape with several threatening probes and in 21 minutes they took the lead when a first-time flick by Calum Murchison allowed John Macrae the opportunity to force the ball over the line at the second attempt. Minutes later, while expecting the traditional Newtonmore riposte, Skye, now with inhibitions lifted, could have gone further ahead but for a fine save by the medal-bespattered Hugh Chisholm. At the other end the Skye defence, with Willie Macrae shining brightly, seemed capable of coping with the best of Badenoch thrusts. They were, however, shown to be fallible when a mistake by Ally Macdonald forced goalkeeper "Bodach" Mackenzie to show his true pedigree in saving from 45-year-old "Tarzan" Ritchie as he swung his way through a rake of Skyemen — always a ticklish task.

In the latter part of the half Newtonmore had most of the pressure as the Skye defence fell back, though Skye were always dangerous on the break and in the minutes before half-time mounted several attacks on the Newtonmore goal. Then, just on the whistle, Norman Macarthur scrambled a goal for Newtonmore.

> With the wind and a 6,000 crowd behind them, the second half and the game overall belonged to Skye. With Caley Maclean becoming an increasingly dominant force in midfield, Macrae and Murchison had narrow misses from long range before Skye restored their lead in 53 minutes with a close-range goal by the alert and speedy Willie Cowie. In 56 minutes, Norman Macarthur was very close for Newtonmore and five minutes later he was frustrated by an excellent save by "Bodach" Mackenzie in full steam if not smoke! By this time, however, a Skye victory had about it a degree of inevitability and this was underlined in 65 minutes when substitute Willie Mackinnon provided a satisfactory Skye finish to a goalmouth stramash. Nevertheless, there still remained something of high quality to savour and, appropriately, who should it come from but the magnificent Willie Cowie. Strangely subdued for most of the match, he picked up a bouncing pass from the wing, flicked it into the air and smashed in a volley which gave no chance even to a goalkeeper of the calibre of Hugh Chisholm. That was in 71 minutes but it proved to be a fitting finale to a grand occasion which cannot do anything else but good for the whole of shinty. Man of the match was Skye's centre half-back, Willie Macrae. The splendid Camanachd trophy and a magnum of whisky were presented by Peter Cullen of Glenmorangie Distilleries to Skye captain Caley Maclean who will, no doubt, not be lacking advice as to how to combine the two!

Delayed by the formal post-match festivities in Fort William, the victorious Skye team didn't arrive home until around 1am the following morning to find the supporters who had arrived long before them, and those who had been forced to stay at home, still thronging the village square to greet them. There was no welcoming volley from the rifles of the Volunteers, certainly, but a peal of church bells served equally well, and the Glencoe never inched in to the pier more carefully than their coach inched through the cheering mass of humanity in the square. And as the players stepped down from the coach clutching their trophy, much as their forebears of almost a century ago had stepped ashore from the Glencoe clutching another trophy, the people rose to them — a community welded together by the victory of its heroes.

The victorious Skye team with the long-sought Camanachd Cup after the match. Unfortunately Willie Macrae (left), awarded the Albert Smith Medal as "Man of the Match" is absent from the group — he was being interviewed by radio and television at the time. Shown with the cup are: Back, l-r, Duncan Macdougall, John "Bodach" Mackenzie, Gerry Ackroyd (trainer), Andy Maclean, Ewen "Crossal" Mackinnon, Donnie "Digg" Macdonald, Calum Murchison, John Macrae, Willie Cowie, Ross Cowie (manager). Front, l-r, John Mackenzie, David Pringle, Ally "Stenscholl" Macdonald, Willie Mackinnon, Cally Maclean (captain), John "Slippy" Finlayson, John Angus Gillies, Peter Gordon.

The shinty "pedigrees" of some members of the team stretch back to the early years of the century and, indeed, to the first Skye team which played Beauly in 1895. Duncan Macdougall is a grandson of Ewen Macdougall, pre-World War I goalkeeper; Andy Maclean is a son of Cally Laban of Skye and Glasgow Skye fame; Calum Murchison is a son of Lachie Chailein; the Cowie brothers are sons of Willie Cowie, grandsons of Angus Mackinnon and great-grandsons of Billy Ross who played in 1895; Willie Mackinnon is also a grandson of Angus Mackinnon and great grandson of Billy Ross; Cally Maclean is a son of Ewen Maclean of the post-World War II era; and Slippy Finlayson's grandfather played for Skye and Glasgow Skye. The youngsters pictured on a later page show such lines continue.

Right: Donnie "Digg" Macdonald, a key man in the Skye Camanachd line-up for almost 20 years.

Left: Willie Cowie in action. He was voted "Scottish Player of the Year" in 1990, the first time such an award was made. He had previously been "North Player of the Year".

Any easy assumption that such trophies once won are easily held from year to year ever after was dispelled during the two subsequent seasons. But even if the team slipped from that single peak of excellence and achievement that the Camanachd Cup represents, no calamitous downfall has occurred, and the club is better placed than at any time in its previous history to regain the height again. The work done since 1969 has led to the most continuous period of stability and expansion that shinty in Skye has ever known. The future of the sport in the community depends on the involvement of youth in it and with almost all of Skye's primary schools now actively involved in providing coaching facilities that future looks secure. But the history of shinty in the community in the last hundred years shows how precarious its existence can be in a sparsely populated area which is ever prone to the loss of too many of its young people to the wider world. In a sense the health of shinty has been a measure of the health of the community. Twice it has been stopped by the holocaust of total war. On many occasions it has been brought to its knees by economic pressures, by the need to leave the island in search of employment. That has been a recurrent factor over the past century and in a fragile economy could easily recur again.

Shinty and Skye Camanachd have also given much to the people of Skye. More than any other activity and more than any other organisation they have provided them with a tangible focus for their communal identity. *Guma fada mhaireas sin* — Long may that last.

Stars of the Future

Skye Camanachd committee, 1991-92, Back row, l-r; Willie Mackinnon, John Finlayson, Willie Macrae, Ross Cowie (manager), John Macrae, Donald Martin,
Front row, l-r; Alistair Bruce (treasurer), John Nicolson, Mrs Margaret Macpherson (chieftain), Kenny Mackay (president), Donald Mackinnon, Archie Macdonald (secretary).

Honorary vice-presidents of Sky Camanachd. Back row, l-r; Neil John MacFarlane, Jimmy Dewar, Donald Angie Macleod, Donald Munro, Billy Mackinnon, Norman Macleod, Donald Michie, Ian Macfarlane,
Front row, l-r; Sorley MacLean, Calum Nicolson, Hamish Macintyre, Mrs Margaret Macpherson (chieftain), Kenny Mackay (president), Mrs Flora Maclean, Alasdair Macleod, John Angus Morrison and John Mackinnon, Bernisdale, were unable to be present.